How Lucky

Deconstructing the Myth of Meritocra

By Joseph Hover

HOW LUCKY ARE YOU? DECONSTRUCTING THE MYTH OF MERITOCRACY, HARD WORK AND WINNING IN LIFE

First edition. October 5, 2024.

ISBN: 979-8227882257

Written by Joseph Hover.

Also by Joseph Hover

The Art Of Survival Navigation: Finding Your Way In The Wilderness
The Case Against Procreation: Antinatalism in Modern Discourse
How Lucky Are You? Deconstructing the Myth of Meritocracy, Hard Work
and Winning in Life

Table of Contents

Chapter 1: The Myth of Meritocracy 1

Chapter 2: The Psychology of Luck Perception 19

Chapter 3: Quantifying Luck: Statistical Insights 31

Chapter 4: The Lottery of Birth 47

Chapter 5: Redefining Success: Beyond Personal Control 57

Chapter 6: Fostering a Compassionate Society.. 61

Chapter 7: The Role of Talent and Skill.. 71

Chapter 8: The Intersection of Luck and Effort.. 81

Chapter 9: Managing Anxiety Related to Unpredictability 85

Chapter 10: Finding Fulfillment Amidst Uncertainty 87

Chapter 11: Replicating Success and Overcoming Obstacles 89

Chapter 1: The Myth of Meritocracy

Chapter 1.1: Historical and Cultural Origins

This topic has been the subject of much debate and contemplation: the myth of meritocracy. In this chapter, we will delve into the intricate relationship between luck and justice, questioning the widely held belief that success is solely determined by one's merit.

Colleges and universities have been grappling with the challenge of ensuring fairness in their admissions processes, often resorting to increasingly stringent standards aimed at selecting only the most qualified candidates. While this approach may seem reasonable at first glance, it frequently contradicts our intrinsic sense of justice and equity. Different individuals within American society hold varying perspectives on what constitutes a fair process, leading to a pressing need to question whether these admission standards genuinely reflect merit or merely uphold the myth of meritocracy.

For instance, an applicant who has access to resources, such as tutoring or extracurricular activities, may find themselves in a more favorable position than someone with equal talent but fewer opportunities. This disparity raises critical questions about the fairness of a system that places so much emphasis on individual achievement without acknowledging the external factors that contribute to success.

Meritocracy is so prevalent in college admissions. Despite the illusion of a fair and objective process, the truth is that it is often akin to a lottery. Admissions officers may strive to maintain an image of impartiality, but the reality is that decisions are influenced by various factors, including personal biases and institutional preferences. Embracing this truth would not only lead to a more honest appraisal of the system but also force us to confront the significant role that luck plays in our lives.

Many pivotal moments in our lives, such as chance encounters or unexpected opportunities, can dramatically alter the course of our paths. I can confidently say that many pivotal moments in my life were the result of fortuitous circumstances. From chance encounters to unexpected opportunities, luck has undeniably played a substantial role in my personal and professional journey.

This inquiry leads us to a critical consideration: is our success genuinely earned? The reality is often unsettling; luck frequently influences outcomes more than we are willing to acknowledge. This notion undermines our entrenched belief that success stems solely from our abilities, diligence, and merit. We inherently resist the idea that significant facets of our lives are susceptible to the unpredictable nature of chance. However, recognizing this truth is essential for a more nuanced comprehension of the intricacies surrounding success and failure.

As we progress through this book, we will investigate how the illusion of meritocracy is woven into the fabric of our society and how it affects individuals from diverse backgrounds. We will scrutinize the glaring discrepancies between the opportunities available to the affluent compared to those accessible to the underprivileged. By analyzing concrete examples and statistical evidence, we will reveal the systemic biases and structural obstacles that sustain inequality while masquerading as merit-based systems.

Before we dive into these complexities, it's important to confront a fundamental reality: luck significantly influences our lives beyond just our intelligence quotient (IQ). While skill and dedication are essential components of success, they form only a portion of the overall equation. The myth of meritocracy overlooks the numerous talented individuals who toil tirelessly yet fail to reach the same heights of success as those who are more privileged.

If you find yourself in discussions with individuals who firmly assert that success is purely the product of skill and hard work, this chapter may very well provoke a shift in their understanding. It's time to face this uncomfortable reality and recognize the pivotal role that luck plays in shaping our destinies.

- The development of the meritocracy concept

The concept of meritocracy has transformed throughout history, influenced by diverse viewpoints and societal conditions. It arose as a countermeasure to the ingrained inequalities and injustices that characterized traditional social hierarchies and privileges. Meritocracy advocates that individuals ought to receive rewards and opportunities based on their skills, talents, and diligence, rather than their social origins or inherited positions.

The term meritocracy was first introduced by British sociologist and politician Michael Young in his satirical work, "The Rise of the Meritocracy," published in the mid-19th century. Young depicted a grim future where social power and status depended entirely on one's cognitive abilities and accomplishments. Although his intention was to critique the potential downsides of a strictly meritocratic society, it ignited a wider discourse on the advantages and disadvantages of meritocracy itself.

In the 20th century, the idea of meritocracy gained momentum, especially regarding education and employment. As societies transitioned into more industrialized and knowledge-driven economies, the need for skilled and capable individuals intensified. The belief that selection and rewards should be based on merit and qualifications resonated widely, appearing to provide a just and effective means for distributing resources and opportunities.

The discourse around meritocracy also reflects the evolving understanding of knowledge and its accessibility. The traditional view that knowledge acquisition is tied to individual training began to shift, suggesting that knowledge is increasingly externalized and shaped by the context in which individuals operate. This changing perception underscores the complexity of meritocracy as it intertwines with societal changes, such as globalization, technological advancements, and shifting educational paradigms, which can influence who gets to define and determine merit in the first place.

As the notion of meritocracy gained traction, it prompted critical inquiries regarding its genuine nature and consequences. Detractors contended that meritocracy often perpetuates existing disparities and reinforces social hierarchies. They observed that individuals from affluent backgrounds frequently enjoyed enhanced access to resources, education, and opportunities, thus providing them an intrinsic advantage within a meritocratic framework.

This led to a heightened awareness that merit alone does not guarantee fairness or equitable opportunity.

Furthermore, the shortcomings of meritocracy in confronting systemic inequalities became increasingly evident. Strategies rooted in meritocracy that reward past achievements often culminate in the concentration of resources and opportunities among a privileged few, thereby widening the chasm between the wealthy and the impoverished. This phenomenon, referred to as the "Matthew effect," underscores the necessity of exploring alternative methods of resource distribution aimed at maximizing potential and societal impact.

In response to these challenges, there have been efforts to investigate more inclusive and equitable strategies within the meritocratic paradigm. One such concept is the idea of stimulating serendipity, which contests conventional meritocratic approaches by advocating for the allocation of smaller grants to a broader array of individuals instead of concentrating resources among a select few successful candidates. This approach attempts to level the playing field and provide opportunities for those who may not traditionally be favored by meritocratic systems.

Additionally, the discourse surrounding meritocracy raises profound ethical considerations regarding societal obligations and the treatment of individuals who, despite their efforts, do not attain success. Philosopher John Rawls introduced the "veil of ignorance" concept, encouraging individuals to contemplate what kind of society they would advocate for if they were unaware of their own social standing. The ongoing discourse on meritocracy remains a focal point of debate as societies endeavor to create more just systems that maximize potential and extend opportunities to all individuals, irrespective of their backgrounds or circumstances.

- Cultural narratives supporting meritocracy

Cultural narratives that support the concept of meritocracy are deeply embedded in societal values and beliefs, often serving as motivational frameworks that encourage individuals to strive for success. One prominent narrative is the notion that success is primarily a product of hard work and determination. This narrative is commonly illustrated through stories of individuals who have surmounted significant challenges through sheer perseverance. Such tales not only inspire but also reinforce the belief that personal effort is the key to achievement, emphasizing personal responsibility and the idea that individuals can take control of their own destinies.

The American Dream serves as another foundational narrative supporting meritocracy. This narrative proposes that individuals, regardless of their socioeconomic background, can attain success through hard work and determination. The ethos of the American Dream has permeated Western culture and has been disseminated globally, suggesting that upward mobility is possible for anyone willing to put in the effort.

Additionally, the narrative of self-made success is particularly compelling in this type of discourse. Individuals who have ascended from modest beginnings to achieve remarkable success are often venerated in society. These rags-to-riches stories captivate public imagination and reinforce the belief that ambition and drive can lead to significant accomplishments. This narrative solidifies the notion that success is attainable through personal initiative.

Together, these cultural narratives create a compelling framework that supports the concept of meritocracy, offering a vision of a society where rewards are distributed based on individual merit. However, it is essential to critically examine these narratives, as they can sometimes obscure the complexities of systemic inequalities and the varying degrees of access to resources that individuals face in their pursuit of success.

It is crucial to recognize that these narratives can sometimes overshadow the complex realities that individuals face. While the idea of the American Dream posits that success is accessible to all, it often fails to account for the disparities in resources, education, and opportunities that exist among different social groups. The narrative of self-made success, while compelling, can inadvertently reinforce the notion that those who do not achieve success simply lack the necessary drive or ambition, disregarding the role of systemic barriers and external factors that may impede one's journey.

- Historical shifts in perceptions of success and merit

Perceptions of success and merit have undergone significant shifts throughout history, reflecting the evolving values, beliefs, and societal structures of different eras.

In ancient civilizations, success was often attributed to divine favor or luck. The belief that one's achievements were tied to harmony with the gods or good fortune illustrates a fundamental understanding of success that challenges the notion that personal traits, such as talent and hard work, alone lead to achievement. Instead, it suggests that luck plays a far more substantial role than typically acknowledged.

The transition to more organized societal structures marked a pivotal change in how success was perceived. In medieval Europe, for example, success was predominantly determined by birthright. Nobility and wealth were inherited rather than earned, with only a small percentage of the population controlling most resources. During this time, merit was often associated with loyalty to the crown and the church, rather than individual accomplishments. This period exemplified a rigid social hierarchy where success was largely predetermined by one's lineage.

The Industrial Revolution of the 18th and 19th centuries heralded a transformative shift in these perceptions. The emergence of a new middle class began to challenge established norms. Economic success became increasingly linked with entrepreneurial spirit and innovation, suggesting that hard work and intelligence could elevate individuals beyond their social status. This era fostered the idea that meritocratic principles could apply, at least to some extent, enabling individuals to rise based on their capabilities rather than their family background.

However, as societies evolved, the association of success with social status and inherited wealth persisted. The concept of a "naive meritocracy" emerged, which warns against underestimating the role of randomness and luck in achieving success. This perspective questions the traditional belief that the most competent individuals are consistently rewarded, highlighting that success is often influenced by external factors outside an individual's control.

In more contemporary contexts, the narrative of success has shifted toward emphasizing personal agency and individual achievement. The American Dream epitomizes this shift, promoting the idea that anyone can achieve success through hard work and determination, regardless of their background. This narrative has become deeply ingrained in American culture and has influenced global perceptions of success.

Entering the 21st century, the notion of meritocracy has become further entrenched, particularly in capitalist societies. Educational attainment and professional accomplishments are often viewed as primary indicators of merit, reinforcing the belief that success is attainable through diligence and talent. Yet, contemporary studies highlight that unconscious biases related to race, gender, and socioeconomic background continue to play significant roles in hiring and promotion decisions. This suggests that our perceptions of merit and success are still evolving and remain influenced by systemic inequalities.

Chapter 1.2: Challenging the Myth with Real-life Examples

In a society that often attributes success solely to meritocracy, examining the journeys of individuals whose achievements defy conventional explanations reveals the nuanced interplay of luck, circumstances, and personal attributes. These case studies challenge the prevailing belief that success is merely a result of hard work and talent, underscoring the importance of recognizing the often-overlooked role of luck in shaping outcomes.

- Defying meritocratic explanations

The Role of Luck in Achieving Success

Many success narratives focus predominantly on hard work and perseverance, neglecting the serendipitous moments and favorable circumstances that can significantly influence one's path. This oversight creates a misleading narrative, suggesting that anyone can replicate such success through sheer effort alone.

Understanding the impact of luck requires a compassionate perspective that acknowledges factors beyond an individual's control, highlighting the importance of seizing opportunities that arise unexpectedly.

Swapping Lives: Wealthy vs. Impoverished

The thought experiment of swapping the lives of the wealthy with those living in poverty starkly illustrates the role of luck in life trajectories. Wealthy individuals often maintain that success is achievable through hard work, but when faced with the harsh realities of poverty, their assumptions are challenged. This exercise underscores the significant ways in which luck and circumstance shape one's opportunities and outcomes. The contrast between the two groups serves to dismantle the notion that success is solely a result of personal attributes, reaffirming that luck plays a pivotal role in determining life chances.

The Distribution of Resources and Maximizing Potential

The critique of the traditional meritocratic approach to resource distribution reveals how meritocratic strategies often perpetuate inequality. The research by Jean-Michel Fortin and David Currie illustrates that larger grants do not necessarily correlate with significant discoveries, suggesting that a more equitable distribution of resources could foster greater overall impact. This finding prompts a reconsideration of meritocratic models that prioritize past success, advocating instead for approaches that maximize potential across a broader spectrum of individuals.

By embracing a more nuanced perspective that recognizes the limitations of a strictly meritocratic narrative, we can cultivate a deeper understanding of achievement that encompasses the myriad factors influencing success. Acknowledging the role of luck and external circumstances not only enriches our comprehension of individual journeys but also encourages a more clear approach to fostering potential in this world.

- The role of luck in pivotal moments of success stories

Luck is often perceived as a mysterious force that significantly influences the defining moments in success narratives. This concept raises important questions about the nature of success: to what extent is it shaped by luck? Is it purely coincidental, or is there a deeper mechanism at work? Analyzing the role of luck in success stories reveals varying viewpoints and insights.

To understand luck, we must first define it. According to psychologist Richard Wiseman, luck is largely a matter of perspective. His research indicates that individuals who identify as lucky tend to maintain an optimistic outlook, which allows them to recognize opportunities where others might see obstacles. This perspective resonates with the Law of Attraction, as articulated in Rhonda Byrne's "The Secret," which underscores the importance of positive thinking in attracting success and opportunities.

However, the question remains: is luck simply a matter of perception? Some contend that luck is closely intertwined with other elements like talent, skill, and hard work. Society frequently operates under the belief that success stems solely from individual traits. Publications such as Success, Forbes, Inc., and Entrepreneur regularly feature the journeys of successful figures, attributing their accomplishments to innate qualities such as talent and perseverance.

The inclination to invest resources in individuals with a proven track record of success, while neglecting those who have not yet achieved, is grounded in the flawed assumption that the most accomplished individuals are also the most capable. This leads to a thought-provoking consideration: could it be that the most successful among us are merely the luckiest?

The argument for luck's pivotal role in success gains further strength when we consider the advantages conferred by background, such as being born into affluence. This disparity emphasizes the need to question the assumption that talent alone guarantees success. It is evident that a disconnect exists in society, where talented individuals may struggle to attain financial success. This inconsistency prompts a reevaluation of the relationship between talent and success.

While it is undeniable that hard work and talent play vital roles in achieving success, luck often acts as a crucial catalyst during key moments. It has the potential to unlock doors, present unforeseen opportunities, and create beneficial circumstances that can propel individuals toward their goals. Ultimately, luck intertwines with talent, skill, and diligence, shaping the diverse pathways to success and underscoring the complexity of achievement in our lives.

Malcolm Gladwell, in "Outliers: The Story of Success," presents a nuanced view of luck's role in achieving success, especially through his "10,000-hour rule." This rule posits that mastery in any field requires approximately 10,000 hours of deliberate practice. While this emphasizes the necessity of commitment and hard work, Gladwell also underscores that luck plays a crucial role in setting the stage for such dedication. Being in the right environment—having access to resources, mentors, or even favorable timing—can significantly influence an individual's ability to invest those hours effectively.

Luck, in this context, can be understood as a blend of preparedness and opportunity. It's not merely a random occurrence; it's about recognizing and acting upon the opportunities presented to us. This perspective aligns closely with Stephen R. Covey's principles in "The 7 Habits of Highly Effective People," where the focus is on being proactive, establishing clear goals, nurturing relationships, and continuously striving for personal growth. By embodying these habits, individuals position themselves to encounter and exploit fortuitous moments more effectively, thereby enhancing their prospects for success.

Research across various disciplines, including psychology, physics, and economics, illuminates the substantial influence of luck on success. It challenges the traditional belief that success can be solely attributed to hard work and talent, emphasizing the importance of being receptive to unexpected opportunities and maintaining an optimistic mindset. While hard work is indispensable, it must be coupled with an awareness of the external factors that can facilitate or hinder one's journey.

- The influence of external factors on career trajectories

External factors significantly shape career trajectories, influencing the paths individuals take throughout their professional lives. Opportunities in a stimulating environment, as well as seemingly trivial factors like one's name or birth month, can profoundly impact an individual's journey. To unpack this complexity, it's essential to explore how luck and opportunity interweave with personal characteristics.

While traits such as passion, perseverance, and creativity undeniably contribute to success, the role of luck and opportunity is often more substantial than we recognize. Research indicates that luck can have a considerable influence on success across various domains, including finance, business, sports, art, music, literature, and science. It's important to clarify that luck does not eclipse hard work or talent; rather, it represents a vital piece of the success puzzle that is frequently overlooked.

A pivotal study by Italian physicists Alessandro Pluchino and Andrea Raspisarda, along with economist Alessio Biondo, offers critical insights into the intersection of luck and talent in career success. Their innovative "toy mathematical model" simulates the career trajectories over a 40-year work life, illustrating how randomness—or luck—shapes the outcomes of individuals' careers. The findings challenge the widely held notion of a purely meritocratic society, suggesting that success is not solely the result of hard work and talent but is significantly influenced by chance.

This research prompts us to reconsider how we allocate resources and recognize success in society. It raises pertinent questions about whether the wealthy and successful genuinely contribute to societal advancement or primarily serve their interests. Through their model, Pluchino and colleagues emphasize the impact of luck, highlighting that many individuals might achieve success through circumstances beyond their control, rather than through a straightforward merit-based system.

The implications of these findings are profound, suggesting that our understanding of success must expand to incorporate the nuances of external influences. External factors such as country of residence and income distribution profoundly influence income disparities, accounting for approximately half of the differences in income among individuals globally. This statistic alone underscores the importance of considering the broader socio-economic context when analyzing career trajectories.

Moreover, the influence of seemingly unrelated factors on career success reveals the subtle ways biases and perceptions can shape professional outcomes. For instance, individuals with last names that appear earlier in the alphabet are statistically more likely to receive tenure at prestigious academic departments. This phenomenon illustrates how arbitrary factors, such as name order, can significantly impact career advancement opportunities. Similarly, the inclusion of middle initials can enhance positive perceptions of an individual's intellectual capabilities, while individuals with names that are easy to pronounce often receive more favorable evaluations compared to those with complex names. These findings emphasize that subtle biases can create an uneven playing field in professional settings, impacting the career trajectories of individuals based on characteristics that have no bearing on their actual abilities or contributions.

Gender also plays a critical role in shaping career outcomes, as seen in the case of females with traditionally masculine-sounding names who tend to achieve greater success in legal professions. This phenomenon highlights the pervasive nature of gender biases and stereotypes, suggesting that even the perception of a name can influence professional success.

In light of these insights, it becomes clear that external factors—including luck, socio-economic context, personal characteristics, and biases—significantly shape career trajectories. While personal attributes such as talent, hard work, and perseverance are undeniably important, they are insufficient on their own to account for the disparities we observe in career success.

Chapter 1.3: Societal Impacts of the Meritocracy Myth

In today's society, the concept of meritocracy has become deeply ingrained in our collective consciousness. Meritocracy promises that success and social status are achieved solely through one's abilities, talents, and hard work. It suggests that those who are the most deserving will rise to the top, while those who are less capable will remain at the bottom. On the surface, this idea seems fair and just, offering hope and motivation to individuals striving for success. However, the societal impacts of the meritocracy myth are far more complex and profound than they initially appear.

The notion of meritocracy has been perpetuated by institutions such as education, employment, and wealth distribution systems. These systems are designed to reward individuals based on their perceived merit, often measured through academic achievements, professional accomplishments, and financial success. The belief in meritocracy has led to the creation of competitive environments where individuals are constantly striving to outperform others in order to secure their place in society.

One of the key societal impacts of the meritocracy myth is the perpetuation of inequality. While meritocracy suggests that everyone has an equal opportunity to succeed, the reality is far from this ideal. Those who are born into privilege and wealth often have greater opportunities and resources at their disposal, giving them a head start in the race for success. Conversely, individuals from disadvantaged backgrounds face numerous barriers and systemic biases that hinder their upward mobility, regardless of their abilities.

The meritocracy myth also creates a culture of individualism and competition, where success is often measured in terms of personal achievements and material wealth. This hyper-focus on individual success can lead to a lack of empathy and a disregard for the collective well-being of society. It fosters a mindset that prioritizes personal gain over the needs of others, perpetuating a cycle of inequality and social division.

Moreover, the belief in meritocracy can have detrimental effects on mental health and well-being. The constant pressure to prove one's worth and compete with others can lead to high levels of stress, anxiety, and burnout. Individuals may feel inadequate and unworthy if they are unable to meet the unrealistic standards set by the meritocracy myth. This can have profound implications for individuals' self-esteem and overall quality of life.

In recent years, there has been a growing body of research challenging the validity of the meritocracy myth. Studies have shown that factors such as luck, privilege, and social networks play a significant role in determining an individual's success.

As we delve deeper into the societal impacts of the meritocracy myth, it becomes evident that the consequences are far-reaching and multifaceted. In the following chapters, we will explore the various dimensions of the meritocracy myth and its societal impacts. We will delve into the role of education, employment, and wealth distribution systems in perpetuating inequality. We will examine the psychological and emotional toll of living in a meritocratic society.

- How belief in meritocracy shapes societal attitudes and policies

Meritocracy is often lauded as a fair system where individuals are rewarded based on their efforts. However, this idealized notion can obscure the complexities of reality. The question remains: does meritocracy truly exist in our society, and do all individuals genuinely have equal opportunities to succeed based solely on their capabilities? I contend that the concept of meritocracy fails to account for a myriad of external factors that influence individual outcomes, including luck, systemic biases, and socio-economic conditions.

At its core, meritocracy implies that hard work and talent are the primary determinants of success. Yet, research indicates that seemingly trivial factors, such as a person's last name or the pronunciation of their name, can significantly influence perceptions of their competence and opportunities in professional settings.

Moreover, the belief in meritocracy can inadvertently reinforce societal inequalities. This phenomenon, often referred to as the "Matthew effect," suggests that those who are already successful are more likely to receive additional opportunities and resources, thereby widening the gap between the haves and the have-nots. As a result, the rich continue to get richer while the poor face increasing barriers to advancement, perpetuating a cycle of privilege and disadvantage. This dynamic challenges the very foundation of the concept we are discussing.

When we prioritize rewarding those who have already achieved success, we risk neglecting the potential of a broader pool of individuals who may not have had the same opportunities but possess the talent and drive to contribute meaningfully. Therefore, it begs the question: should we continue to allocate resources to a select few or consider a more equitable distribution that could foster greater potential across a diverse populace?

This requires us to critically evaluate the strategies used to assign honors, funds, and rewards in our society. The meritocratic system, as it stands, fails to recognize external influences, thus perpetuating an illusion of equality that is not reflected in reality.

- The psychological effects on individuals striving for success

The psychological effects on individuals striving for success is a topic that has fascinated me for years as an observer of human behavior. We live in a society that places great value on achievement and success, and it's no wonder that many individuals are driven to pursue their goals with unwavering determination. But what are the psychological consequences of this relentless pursuit?

The acknowledgment of luck's role in success fundamentally challenges the entrenched belief that hard work and intelligence are the sole determinants of outcomes. This recognition not only reshapes our understanding of achievement but also illuminates the often-overlooked dynamics of opportunity and timing in the pursuit of success. It compels us to reflect on the multifaceted nature of achievement and encourages a more compassionate perspective toward those who, despite their diligence, find themselves thwarted by unfavorable circumstances. This understanding is vital in preventing the self-blame that individuals frequently impose upon themselves when they perceive failure, prompting a recognition of the external factors at play in their journeys.

At the crux of this discussion is the interplay between perspective and luck. Individuals who view themselves as fortunate often possess a broader outlook, enabling them to identify and capitalize on opportunities that others might overlook. This perspective can significantly influence their ability to navigate the complexities of success. The traditional narrative surrounding success, which often prioritizes meritocratic values, fails to account for the serendipitous encounters and chance events that can alter the trajectory of an individual's life. Luck can serve as a pivotal element that tips the scales of success, suggesting that hard work and talent, while indispensable, do not function in isolation.

Moreover, the underappreciation of luck in the discourse surrounding success perpetuates a detrimental cycle where resources and rewards are disproportionately allocated to those who have already achieved success. Consequently, this disparity underscores the necessity of expanding our understanding of success beyond mere personal effort and intelligence, recognizing that it is often a mosaic of various factors, including luck.

The psychological ramifications of acknowledging luck's influence are profound and multifaceted. For many pursuing success, the realization that external factors significantly shape outcomes can be both liberating and disheartening. On one hand, this awareness alleviates the burden of self-blame that commonly accompanies failure, fostering a more compassionate self-perception. It encourages individuals to adopt a proactive mindset, emphasizing the importance of building relationships and seizing opportunities. Conversely, the randomness inherent in luck may induce feelings of powerlessness, particularly among those who have exerted considerable effort yet continue to face barriers to success. This duality reflects the complexities of the human experience in striving for achievement.

To effectively navigate this intricate landscape, individuals must strike a balance between recognizing the influence of luck and maintaining a proactive approach toward their aspirations. Embracing a more expansive perspective empowers individuals to cultivate resilience and adaptability in the face of unpredictability.

- Long-term societal consequences of overlooking luck

The long-term societal consequences of overlooking luck in the context of success are indeed profound and multifaceted. When we fail to acknowledge the role of luck, we risk reinforcing a distorted perception of meritocracy that can shape resource distribution and influence the well-being of individuals and communities.

At the heart of this issue lies the widespread belief that success is the sole result of hard work and talent. This narrative, while empowering to some, can lead to a detrimental stigma against those who do not achieve similar outcomes. By attributing success exclusively to personal effort, we overlook the myriad external factors—timing, circumstance, and sheer chance—that can significantly influence one's trajectory. Consequently, individuals facing adverse conditions may be unjustly blamed for their lack of success, perpetuating social divisions and deepening inequalities.

Research simulations, such as those that track career evolution over a prolonged period, illustrate that even the most talented individuals can experience wildly divergent outcomes based on luck. This evidence underlines the arbitrary nature of success and challenges the meritocratic ideal that those who succeed have simply "earned" their achievements.

The implications for resource distribution are particularly concerning. In a meritocratic framework, the prevailing assumption is that wealth is justly apportioned to those who have worked for it. However, this view neglects the reality that luck plays a critical role in determining who gets what opportunities. This creates a vicious cycle where the successful continue to accrue advantages, while those who struggle are further marginalized.

Moreover, the failure to recognize luck can erode empathy and compassion within society. When individuals perceive their success as solely a product of their own efforts, they may be less likely to support initiatives aimed at helping others. This lack of understanding can lead to resistance against social safety nets or policies designed to mitigate systemic inequalities. Such attitudes can perpetuate a cycle of disadvantage, making it increasingly difficult for those in less favorable positions to escape their circumstances.

Acknowledging luck does not diminish the value of hard work and talent; rather, it enriches our perspective by recognizing how external factors can shape outcomes. This shift in understanding could foster greater empathy and support for policies aimed at leveling the playing field and addressing systemic inequities.

Chapter 2: The Psychology of Luck Perception

Chapter 2.1: Psychological Theories on Luck

- Overview of theories like the Law of Attraction

The Law of Attraction (LoA) posits that our thoughts and intentions wield the power to shape our life experiences, suggesting that positive thoughts can manifest positive outcomes while negative thoughts can lead to adverse circumstances. This compelling narrative gained traction largely due to Rhonda Byrne's "The Secret," which popularized the idea that individuals can actively create their realities through the power of their mindset. However, the implications of such beliefs extend far beyond mere positive thinking; they redefine how individuals approach personal growth and achievement.

One of the core tenets of the Law of Attraction is visualization. Proponents advocate for individuals to vividly envision their desired outcomes, believing that such clarity and focus will compel the universe to align circumstances in their favor. This practice can be likened to the cognitive strategies outlined in Stephen R. Covey's "The 7 Habits of Highly Effective People," where principles such as goal setting and proactive behavior are emphasized. Covey's framework aligns with the LoA by underscoring the importance of a proactive mindset, which inherently attracts success and opportunities through intentional action.

Gratitude is another crucial aspect of the Law of Attraction. Practitioners are encouraged to express thankfulness for existing blessings, which is believed to foster an abundance mindset and attract further positivity. This emphasis on gratitude can enhance emotional well-being and resilience, promoting a constructive outlook that empowers individuals to navigate challenges with a more optimistic lens. Such a mindset shift can be transformative, leading to increased motivation and a sense of control over one's life.

However, the Law of Attraction is not without its critics. Skeptics argue that its principles lack scientific validation and are often grounded in anecdotal evidence. This critique raises questions about the balance between belief and empirical evidence in the pursuit of success. Detractors contend that attributing success solely to mindset overlooks the critical roles of systemic factors, external circumstances, and, crucially, the element of luck. This critique is particularly poignant when considering that some individuals face significant barriers that cannot be overcome through positive thinking alone.

Nonetheless, many individuals find intrinsic value in the principles of the Law of Attraction, utilizing them as tools for personal development. The focus on positive thinking, visualization, and gratitude can serve to cultivate a mindset that encourages resilience and proactivity. While the theory emphasizes intention, it does not negate the necessity of action. For the LoA to be effective, individuals must not only visualize their goals but also engage in tangible steps toward achieving them.

This fusion of mindset and action presents a more holistic approach to personal growth, blending the power of belief with the practicality of effort. By fostering positivity, clarity of intention, and gratitude, individuals may find themselves more motivated and equipped to pursue their goals.

Ultimately, whether one subscribes to the Law of Attraction or not, the underlying principles of cultivating a positive mindset and taking proactive steps toward goals can undoubtedly contribute to personal achievement and well-being.

- Cognitive biases influencing luck perception

Cognitive biases significantly shape our perceptions of luck, success, and failure, influencing how we interpret events and outcomes in our lives. Understanding these biases can provide valuable insights into human behavior and decision-making.

One of the most pervasive cognitive biases affecting our perception of luck is hindsight bias. This phenomenon causes individuals to believe that they could have predicted an event's outcome after the fact. For example, after a major sports event, fans might claim they "knew" the winning team would prevail, attributing their success to foresight rather than luck. This bias can lead to an inflated sense of control over outcomes, distorting our understanding of luck's role and potentially affecting future decisions, as we may fail to recognize the unpredictable nature of events.

The availability heuristic also plays a crucial role in shaping our beliefs about luck. Our judgments are often influenced by readily available information, which can skew our perception. When we hear numerous stories of lottery winners or successful entrepreneurs attributing their achievements to luck, we may overestimate the impact of chance on success. Conversely, we might overlook the many individuals who struggle despite similar efforts but don't receive the same media attention. This selective emphasis distorts our understanding of luck and success, leading us to believe that extraordinary outcomes are solely the result of fortunate circumstances.

Anchoring bias further complicates our perceptions. Individuals often rely heavily on the first piece of information they encounter, which can color their views on luck. For instance, if someone experiences a run of good luck early in their career, they might anchor their self-image around being inherently lucky. This fixed mindset can prevent them from recognizing the role of hard work, skill, and even the influence of external factors like opportunity and timing, which are often overlooked due to their focus on initial experiences.

Confirmation bias exacerbates these issues by compelling individuals to seek out information that confirms their existing beliefs while dismissing contradictory evidence. When individuals believe luck plays a significant role in success, they may only pay attention to stories that support this idea, ignoring examples where success is attributed to hard work or systemic factors. This bias reinforces existing perceptions and can create a narrow understanding of the complex interplay between luck and success, hindering a more nuanced exploration of both concepts.

The framing effect also significantly influences how we perceive and interpret luck. The way information is presented can shape our judgments and attitudes. For example, if a successful individual attributes their achievements to luck, it may foster a perception of humility, while someone who dismisses luck in favor of personal effort may come across as arrogant. This framing can impact societal attitudes toward success and luck, influencing how individuals view their own experiences and the narratives they create around achievement.

By critically examining these cognitive biases, we can refine our understanding of luck, success, and failure and develop more effective decision-making strategies. Acknowledging these biases allows individuals to adopt a more balanced perspective, recognizing the interplay of luck, effort, and external factors in shaping outcomes while fostering a mindset that values adaptability and resilience in the face of uncertainty.

- The psychology behind superstitions and luck rituals

Superstitions and luck rituals have pervaded human culture for centuries, deeply embedded in our societal fabric and individual psyches. They manifest in various forms, from avoiding black cats to carrying lucky charms or engaging in specific rituals before significant events. The motivations behind these seemingly irrational behaviors are multifaceted, intertwining psychological needs with social influences.

Central to the allure of superstitions is our inherent desire for control in an unpredictable world. Life's uncertainties can be daunting, prompting individuals to seek methods to mitigate the chaos surrounding them. Engaging in superstitious practices provides a semblance of control, allowing individuals to feel as if they can influence outcomes, even if such influence exists only symbolically. This act of ritualization instills a sense of order and predictability, effectively reducing anxiety and enhancing our perceived mastery over life's events.

The placebo effect further underscores the psychological power of belief intrinsic to superstitions. Our perceptions shape our reality; when individuals genuinely believe in the efficacy of a ritual or charm, its psychological implications can be significant. This belief can bolster self-confidence, enhance performance, and even promote psychological well-being. For example, athletes often engage in superstitions as a way to harness this belief, demonstrating how mindset can substantially impact physical outcomes.

Moreover, these rituals serve as coping mechanisms in the face of adversity. They provide comfort, acting as psychological anchors in turbulent times. By offering a framework of hope and reassurance, superstitions help individuals navigate uncertainty. This psychological scaffolding becomes particularly vital in challenging circumstances, as the belief in a positive outcome can motivate resilience and optimism.

Cognitive biases also play a crucial role in the persistence of superstitions. Our brains are wired to recognize patterns and draw connections, often leading to the "illusion of control." This cognitive phenomenon compels us to attribute meaning to random events, reinforcing the belief that certain actions or objects can influence outcomes. Such tendencies can perpetuate superstitions, as individuals continue to seek and find correlations in the chaos of life, even when these relationships are purely coincidental.

Social and cultural factors further enrich our understanding of why superstitions endure. Humans are inherently social beings; our beliefs and behaviors are significantly shaped by the norms and practices of those around us. The observation of others engaging in superstitions can foster a collective belief, reinforcing these behaviors within communities. Additionally, cultural narratives and folklore often embed these practices within a societal context, ensuring their transmission across generations.

Despite the tendency to dismiss such practices as irrational, their psychological significance cannot be overlooked. They furnish individuals with comfort, hope, and a semblance of control in an often chaotic existence. As we navigate our lives, it is essential to recognize that engaging in superstitions is not merely about luck; it reflects the complex interplay of human psychology, social influences, and cultural traditions. These elements together highlight the fascinating workings of the human mind and our enduring quest for meaning and stability in an unpredictable world.

Chapter 2.2: Mindset and Perceived Luck

- The role of resilience and optimism in perceived luck

The narratives of individuals who have navigated the complexities of life often illustrate that financial struggles and hardships are not always indicative of an individual's effort or character; rather, they can stem from unfortunate circumstances or being in the wrong place at the wrong time, highlighting a nuanced understanding of success and failure.

Moreover, the resilience demonstrated by individuals in the face of adversity is striking. Those who cultivate an optimistic mindset tend to harness a remarkable ability to perceive opportunities amidst obstacles. While it is undeniable that life's challenges can be daunting, the capacity to adapt to changing circumstances reflects a profound mental and emotional strength.

Yet, it is essential to acknowledge the gravity of truly devastating setbacks, such as the loss of employment, housing, or loved ones. Such experiences can cast shadows that obscure even the faintest glimmers of hope, making it exceedingly difficult to maintain an optimistic outlook. However, even in the bleakest moments, the potential for hope exists, albeit often hidden beneath layers of grief and hardship. It becomes the responsibility of those who have experienced more "green dots"—the fortunate moments of serendipity—to extend a hand to those grappling with adversity. Sharing personal stories, providing encouragement, and reminding others that they are not alone can create a community that fosters resilience. Maybe?

In reflecting on our shared human experience, it is clear that success is rarely achieved in isolation. The most accomplished individuals often attribute their journeys to the support networks composed of friends, family, and mentors who guided them through life's obstacles. This connection emphasizes the importance of creating a society where everyone has a fair chance at success, regardless of their starting point.

As we consider our personal journeys, we must ask ourselves what "green dots" and "red dots" have influenced our paths. Where have we encountered fortune, and where have we faced challenges? How have we responded to these experiences? Have we allowed adversity to define us, or have we harnessed our inner strength to rise above it? The potential for resilience and optimism resides within each of us, waiting to be accessed. Although this may require time and effort to cultivate, it remains an enduring truth that when we tap into our inner fortitude, we open the door to a vast array of possibilities.

Ultimately, the essence of our lives is not dictated by the circumstances we face but by how we choose to confront them. It is a journey defined by the courage to take risks, the wisdom to learn from our experiences, and the resilience to forge ahead, regardless of the challenges that life may present.

- Techniques to foster a luck-enhancing mindset

How can we foster a luck-enhancing mindset? It starts with adopting a growth mindset - the belief that our abilities and circumstances are not fixed, but rather can be developed and improved through hard work and dedication. This mindset shift is crucial, as it allows us to see setbacks not as failures, but as opportunities for growth and learning.

Next, it's about practicing gratitude and positive self-talk. By focusing on the things we're grateful for, and by reframing our inner dialogue to be more encouraging and empowering, we can train our brains to seek out the "green dots" rather than dwelling on the "red dots." This, in turn, can help us recognize and seize the lucky opportunities that arise.

Another important technique is to expand our social circles and seek out diverse perspectives. By connecting with people from different backgrounds and experiences, we can broaden our horizons and gain new insights that can help us navigate the complexities of life. Additionally, fostering strong relationships and building a supportive network can open the door to unexpected opportunities and resources.

Visualization and goal-setting are also powerful tools in the quest for luck. By clearly defining our objectives and mentally rehearsing the steps to achieve them, we can increase our focus, motivation, and resilience. And by breaking down our big goals into smaller, actionable steps, we can build momentum and stay on track, even in the face of challenges.

Finally, it's about cultivating a mindset of continuous learning and improvement. By embracing a spirit of curiosity and a willingness to experiment, we can stay adaptable and open to new possibilities. And by regularly reflecting on our progress and learning from our mistakes, we can hone our skills and increase our chances of success.

At the end of the day, it's not about the cards we're dealt, It's about having the courage to take risks, the wisdom to learn from our mistakes, and the resilience to keep pushing forward, no matter what life throws our way.

Chapter 2.3: Practical Strategies for a Positive Outlook

- Exercises to build a positive mental framework

While it's true that certain events and circumstances are beyond our control, I firmly believe that our mindset and approach can significantly influence the opportunities that come our way. The research outlined previously supports this idea - those who view themselves as "lucky" tend to have a wider perspective and focus on the positive, which in turn attracts more positive experiences.

So, how do we cultivate this elusive "positive mindset"? It's not as simple as snapping our fingers and suddenly becoming an eternal optimist. It takes consistent effort and a willingness to challenge our own thought patterns. But trust me, the payoff is well worth it.

One of the foundational exercises I recommend is the practice of gratitude. Far too often, we get caught up in the daily grind, fixating on the problems and challenges we face. But by taking a step back and consciously acknowledging the blessings in our lives - whether it's the roof over our heads, the food on our table, or the loved ones who support us - we shift our focus to the abundance rather than the scarcity. This simple shift can have a profound impact on our overall outlook and well-being.

Another powerful tool in our mental fitness arsenal is visualization. Imagine, for a moment, your ideal future - what does it look like? How do you feel when you envision yourself achieving your goals and living your dream life? By regularly practicing this mental exercise, we train our brains to recognize and seize the opportunities that align with our vision. It's like a self-fulfilling prophecy, where our thoughts and beliefs shape the reality we experience.

But let's not forget the importance of physical well-being in this equation. After all, our minds and bodies are inextricably linked. Engaging in regular exercise, whether it's a brisk walk, a yoga session, or a high-intensity workout, can have a remarkable effect on our mental state. Not only does it release feel-good endorphins, but it also helps us manage stress and maintain a clear, focused mindset.

And speaking of stress, let's not underestimate the power of mindfulness and meditation. In a world that's constantly bombarding us with stimuli and demands, it's crucial to carve out time for ourselves to simply be present, to quiet the chatter in our minds, and to reconnect with our inner selves. By cultivating this practice, we become better equipped to navigate the ups and downs of life with a sense of calm and equanimity.

Striking a balance between minimizing risks—represented by "red dots"—and embracing opportunities, or "green dots," involves a proactive and strategic mindset. For instance, when considering physical activities, one might minimize the risk of jogging on a busy road by choosing safer environments, such as parks or designated running tracks. This approach not only protects against potential dangers but also allows for the maintenance of an active lifestyle in a more secure setting. Such decisions reflect a thoughtful consideration of risk management while still pursuing personal health goals.

Furthermore, the pursuit of "green dots" through expanding social networks and fostering relationships can yield significant benefits. Engaging with diverse individuals exposes us to new perspectives and insights, which enhance our ability to navigate life's challenges. These interactions are invaluable, as they provide not only opportunities for collaboration but also a deeper understanding of the communities we inhabit. By being mindful of the codes and values within these communities, individuals can create meaningful connections that empower them to embrace opportunities while effectively managing risks.

But perhaps the most important exercise of all is the one that ties everything together: continuous self-improvement. By constantly striving to learn, grow, and expand our horizons, we not only enhance our skills and knowledge but also cultivate a mindset of resilience and adaptability. When we're open to new experiences and willing to step outside our comfort zones, we become better equipped to seize the "green dots" and sidestep the "red dots" that come our way.

The practice of visualization and affirmation serves as a powerful mechanism for rewiring neural pathways and transforming subconscious beliefs. By consistently picturing our successes and affirming our abilities, we engage in cognitive restructuring that mitigates self-doubt and imposter syndrome—two prevalent mental obstacles that hinder personal growth. This technique allows individuals to actively shape their perceptions of self-worth and capability, effectively fostering a more positive mental framework

- Success stories from individuals who shifted their outlook

Success stories abound, illustrating the profound impact a shift in mindset can have on individuals' lives. Among these narratives, we find Michael, a former corporate executive who faced significant challenges, including overwhelming debt and deep-seated depression. His journey to transformation began at a critical juncture when he chose to reassess his life and priorities.

Michael's initial foray into change involved the practices of mindfulness and meditation. These techniques enabled him to cultivate a deeper awareness of his thoughts and emotions, facilitating a clearer understanding of his inner landscape. This introspection paved the way for him to embrace minimalism, allowing him to reduce the clutter in his life—both physically and mentally. By focusing on what truly mattered, he was able to gain clarity and purpose, ultimately leading him to a courageous career transition. He left behind the high-pressure corporate world to become a life coach, a role that now provides him not only financial stability but also profound personal fulfillment. His transformation illustrates a crucial point: the shift in mindset—from one of scarcity and despair to one of abundance and possibility—was key to his success.

Such stories underscore the transformative power of a positive outlook. However, what mechanisms are at play that allow this shift in perspective to catalyze profound change? The answer lies in the complex interplay between our thoughts, emotions, and actions. Adopting a positive mindset is not merely a cursory endeavor; it involves a significant rewiring of the brain's neural pathways. This cognitive restructuring enables individuals to perceive the world through a lens that highlights opportunities rather than obstacles, fostering a sense of optimism that propels them forward.

The cascading effects of this positive shift are noteworthy. With an optimistic mindset, individuals are more inclined to take calculated risks, pursue novel experiences, and persist despite setbacks. This increased resilience often leads to the cultivation of meaningful relationships and a supportive community, further reinforcing the positive changes initiated by their mindset.

Moreover, the tangible outcomes of these mindset shifts are significant. As individuals begin to experience success, they attract more opportunities—these 'green dots"—while effectively navigating the "red dots" of adversity. This creates a self-fulfilling prophecy, where positive beliefs and thoughts shape the reality they encounter, leading to a virtuous cycle of success and fulfillment.

For those feeling trapped in a cycle of negativity or stagnation, the narratives of transformation serve as a beacon of hope. Starting with small, manageable practices can initiate the journey toward a more positive mindset. Engaging with one's dreams and trusting in the potential for positive alignment can ultimately unlock the greatness within.

The journey toward success may not always be straightforward, but the destination—characterized by fulfillment, resilience, and achievement—is undeniably worth the effort.

Chapter 3: Quantifying Luck: Statistical Insights

Chapter 3.1: Measuring the Impact of Luck

Traditionally, we've been conditioned to believe that success is a direct reflection of one's talent and hard work. Society idolizes the "self-made" individual, painting a picture where the most skilled and diligent rise to prominence. But what if there's more to the story?

The role of luck in determining life's outcomes is significantly larger than many of us had anticipated. It's a sobering realization that the randomness of life—those unexpected opportunities and serendipitous moments—can overshadow even the most diligent efforts and innate abilities.

What does this mean for our understanding of meritocracy? If we accept that luck plays a substantial role, we must confront uncomfortable truths about societal structures. Are we truly rewarding the deserving, or are we simply privileging those who happen to find themselves in advantageous situations?

As we navigate through this chapter, we must grapple with the implications of these findings. They challenge the narrative that hard work and talent alone dictate success, urging us to acknowledge the often-overlooked influence of chance.

- Statistical methods used in studying luck

Let's dive into the core findings of an illuminating research. The researchers behind this study astutely identified a disconnect between individual talent and actual success in financial and career terms. We've been conditioned to accept that the most gifted and industrious individuals naturally ascend to the top of the social ladder, but this study shakes that belief to its foundations.

Their replication of the "Pareto Principle" was a key finding: a small elite often holds a disproportionate share of success. In this case, the top 20 achievers captured a staggering 44% of total success, leaving nearly half of the population stuck at their starting point. This stark reality highlights an unsettling truth about how success is distributed.

What's particularly striking is that while talent may be evenly spread across the population, success is not. The researchers uncovered a significant skew, where a select few individuals experience outsized success. Crucially, they attributed this phenomenon more to luck than to talent or hard work. In their simulations, they modeled both "lucky" and "unlucky" events that could dramatically enhance or diminish an individual's success. Those fortunate enough to encounter a greater number of positive chance events surged ahead, often irrespective of their innate abilities.

If success hinges more on serendipity than merit, we must reconsider whether we genuinely understand what luck means. The research indicated that luck's impact is not evenly distributed; it has an exponential effect, meaning that a marginal advantage in luck can lead to disproportionately larger rewards.

Now, you might be pondering the challenge of quantifying something as elusive as "luck." It sounds paradoxical, yet the researchers cleverly tackled this by executing thousands of simulations, allowing them to disentangle the roles of talent, effort, and random chance. This methodological approach provides a robust framework for understanding how much of our success is attributable to factors beyond our control.

The implications are vast. Should we implement measures to level the playing field and mitigate the effects of chance events? Or is that an unattainable ideal? These inquiries are not just academic; they resonate deeply with our values and priorities as a society.

This research has reshaped my own understanding of success. I once held the belief that hard work and talent were the sole determinants of achievement. Now, I realize that a significant element of randomness plays a pivotal role, a factor we've largely overlooked.

So, what do we do with this newfound understanding? It calls for humility and gratitude. We must refrain from harsh judgments against those who haven't "made it," recognizing that their struggles may stem from bad luck rather than personal shortcomings. Conversely, those of us who have found success should express gratitude for the fortunate events that have aided our journeys.

Moreover, this research underscores the necessity for policies that address the disproportionate impact of luck. Perhaps we need a more comprehensive social safety net or a re-evaluation of how we allocate resources and opportunities.

Ultimately, we are all just a roll of the dice away from either soaring success or devastating failure. Shouldn't we strive to tip the scales in favor of everyone?

- Key metrics and indicators of luck's role in success

Let's start by unpacking the key metrics and indicators the researchers used to study the impact of luck. The way they went about this is really quite ingenious.

The core of their model was incorporating not just talent and effort, but also the random chance events that can make or break a person's trajectory. They started by giving each of the 1,000 participants an equal "starting wealth" of 10 units, and then allowed their fortunes to rise and fall over the course of their simulated careers based on a combination of their inherent abilities and a series of random positive and negative "luck events."

These luck events were designed to either double or halve a person's success, respectively, with the probability of encountering them determined by a normal distribution. So some individuals would be "luckier" than others, encountering more of the positive events that propelled them forward.

By running this simulation thousands of times, the researchers were able to start quantifying just how much of an impact these random chance occurrences had compared to the participants' underlying talents and efforts. And the results are nothing short of eye-opening.

To quantify this, the researchers looked at a number of key metrics. One was the "Gini coefficient," a measure of income inequality that ranges from 0 (perfect equality) to 1 (maximum inequality). In their simulations, the Gini coefficient ended up being around 0.6 - significantly higher than the real-world value of around 0.45, suggesting that luck is exacerbating inequality to an even greater degree than we observe in the actual economy.

They also looked at the ratio of the wealth of the top 10% to the bottom 10% - a common measure of economic disparity. In their model, this ratio ended up being around 30, compared to a real-world value of around 9. Again, this points to luck playing a much bigger role in driving extreme wealth concentration than we typically account for.

Another interesting metric the researchers tracked was the "success rate" - the percentage of participants who ended up achieving a certain level of wealth or career status. Across their thousands of simulations, they found that only around 20% of the population ever reached the top 20% in terms of success. And the vast majority of those high-achievers owed their position more to luck than to any innate talent or effort.

Perhaps most mind-bending of all, the researchers found that the correlation between a participant's initial talent and their final level of success was actually quite low - around 0.3. This means that talent alone explains less than 10% of the variation in outcomes. The rest is down to the random twists and turns of fate!

Chapter 3.2: Analysis of Industry-specific Data

- Finance: The role of market conditions and timing

Okay, let's dive into the fascinating world of finance and how market conditions and timing play a crucial role in success. It's not just about raw talent or a killer instinct; it's about understanding the ebb and flow of the market and making the right moves at the right time. Think of it like surfing. You can be the most skilled surfer on the planet, but if you're not catching the right wave at the right moment, you're not going to be riding any barrels.

Let's start with the big picture. The financial markets are constantly in flux, driven by a complex interplay of economic indicators, investor sentiment, geopolitical events, and even random chance. Think of it like a giant, unpredictable machine with a million moving parts.

Market Conditions:

Economic Indicators: These are the bread and butter of financial analysis. Things like GDP growth, inflation rates, interest rates, and unemployment figures all provide valuable insights into the overall health of the economy. A strong economy generally leads to higher stock prices, while a weak economy can cause markets to tumble.

Investor Sentiment: This is the collective mood of investors, which can be influenced by a variety of factors, including news headlines, economic data, and even social media trends. When investors are optimistic, they tend to buy stocks, driving prices up. When they're pessimistic, they sell, pushing prices down.

Geopolitical Events: Wars, political instability, and trade disputes can all have a significant impact on financial markets. For example, the 2008 financial crisis was triggered in part by the collapse of the housing market in the United States, which was exacerbated by the global financial crisis.

Random Chance: Let's face it, sometimes things just happen. Think of the "Black Swan" events, those unpredictable and highly impactful events that can shake the markets. The COVID-19 pandemic is a prime example. These events can be difficult to predict and often have a significant impact on market sentiment and investor behavior.

Timing:

Market Cycles: Markets tend to move in cycles, with periods of growth followed by periods of decline. Understanding these cycles can help investors make better decisions about when to buy and sell. For example, if you're investing in a market that's nearing the end of a bull market (a period of sustained growth), you might want to consider selling some of your holdings and taking profits. On the other hand, if the market is in a bear market (a period of decline), you might want to buy stocks at a discount, hoping to capitalize on the eventual rebound.

Entry and Exit Points: Timing your entry and exit points is crucial for maximizing returns. If you buy a stock at the wrong time, you could end up losing money. Conversely, if you sell at the right time, you can lock in your profits. This is where research, analysis, and a bit of intuition come into play.

Risk Tolerance: Your risk tolerance is another important factor to consider when timing your investments. If you're a risk-averse investor, you might want to avoid investing in volatile markets or stocks that are prone to large swings in price. On the other hand, if you're comfortable with risk, you might be willing to invest in more volatile markets or stocks that have the potential for higher returns.

The Role of Institutional Money Managers:

Now, let's talk about those institutional money managers, the folks who manage large sums of money for pension funds, insurance companies, and other institutions. They're often seen as the "experts" in the financial world, and their decisions can have a significant impact on market movements.

But even these experts aren't immune to the influence of market conditions and timing. As the data suggests, institutional money managers tend to perform best in their mid-40s. Why is that? It's likely a combination of factors:

- Experience: By their mid-40s, these managers have accumulated years of experience navigating the ups and downs of the market. They've seen it all, from bull markets to bear markets, and they've learned from their mistakes.

- Network: Over time, they've built a strong network of contacts in the industry, giving them access to valuable information and insights.

- Confidence: With experience comes confidence, which can be a valuable asset in the high-pressure world of finance. Confident managers are more likely to make bold decisions and stick to their convictions, even when the market is volatile.

- Business: Startup success and failure rates

In the vibrant yet tumultuous world of startups, where dreams are born and fortunes can be made or lost in the blink of an eye, aspiring entrepreneurs face an array of challenges. The sobering reality is that a staggering 70% to 90% of startups fail, presenting an uphill battle for those daring enough to venture into this arena.

However, understanding the dynamics of this landscape—particularly the role of luck, the importance of learning from failures, strategic funding, and timing—can empower entrepreneurs to navigate these treacherous waters more effectively.

Let's first address the daunting failure rates head-on. It's crucial to recognize that failure is often not just a possibility but a near certainty for many startups. However, what distinguishes successful entrepreneurs from those who struggle is not merely the absence of failure but their response to it. Failures can serve as invaluable learning experiences, offering insights into market demands, operational inefficiencies, and even personal resilience. This perspective aligns with the notion that failure is not the opposite of success, but rather a stepping stone toward it. Many renowned entrepreneurs have experienced multiple setbacks before achieving their breakthroughs, highlighting the necessity to fail smart—learning quickly, pivoting when necessary, and avoiding the repetition of past mistakes.

It is tempting to dismiss luck as a mere excuse for failure; however, research indicates that serendipity can significantly influence startup success. Success is not solely a product of rigorous planning and execution but can also hinge on fortuitous circumstances—being in the right place at the right time, meeting the right people, or capitalizing on emerging trends. Thus, while one cannot control luck, one can position themselves to seize opportunities when they arise. This requires being well-prepared, possessing a robust business plan, and maintaining an agile mindset that allows for quick adaptations.

Funding is another critical component for aspiring entrepreneurs. While it is common knowledge that many startups fail due to capital shortages, it is equally important to understand that more funding does not always equate to greater success. In fact, an influx of capital can lead to complacency and inefficient spending, causing startups to lose focus. Therefore, entrepreneurs should adopt a strategic approach to funding—raising only what is necessary and prioritizing the cultivation of meaningful relationships with investors who offer not just financial backing but also valuable expertise and connections.

Timing, too, plays a pivotal role in a startup's trajectory. A well-crafted product can flounder if introduced to a market that is unprepared or uninterested. Conversely, even a subpar offering can thrive if it enters the market at the right moment. Historical examples abound: Uber's rise coincided with the proliferation of smartphones, enabling the ride-sharing model to flourish as it never could have before.

In conclusion, aspiring entrepreneurs must approach the startup landscape with both courage and realism. Recognizing the high likelihood of failure, embracing the learning opportunities inherent in setbacks, strategically seeking funding, and remaining aware of market timing can significantly enhance their chances of success.

- Sports and Arts: The unpredictability of fame and success

Numerous studies have illuminated the startling reality that, in competitive fields such as sports and the arts, luck often exerts a far greater influence than we would care to acknowledge. We're talking about the type of luck that can instantly elevate an unknown individual into the spotlight or, conversely, cause a promising career to falter in an instant.

To clarify, this is not to undermine the importance of talent. It is undeniable that one cannot ascend to the ranks of world-class musicians or elite athletes without exceptional skill and effort. However, the pivotal moment comes when individuals reach a certain baseline of competence; at this juncture, the competitive landscape becomes remarkably level. In the upper echelons of any professional domain, individuals are nearly all supremely talented and have invested significant time honing their craft. Thus, what distinguishes the shining stars from those who merely linger in the shadows often boils down to serendipity—being in the right place at the right time, catching the attention of a vital figure, or seizing that one fortuitous opportunity that can set everything in motion.

Let's take the world of sports as an illustrative example. You would think that athletics, with its concrete metrics and measurable outcomes, would be a meritocratic domain governed solely by hard work and innate ability. Yet, even within this realm, luck plays a significant role. For instance, the NFL draft can be likened to a game of chance. Despite exhaustive scouting efforts and extensive analysis, predicting which college athlete will evolve into the next gridiron legend can often feel like consulting a Magic 8 Ball. Moreover, securing a favorable position in a team's system, matched with an adept coach, can make all the difference. A quarterback might flourish under one system while floundering in another, underscoring how timing and a sprinkle of luck can shape athletic careers.

Transitioning to the arts, the unpredictability becomes even more pronounced. The narrative of the struggling artist who achieves fame is often romanticized, yet the reality is typically much more chaotic and random. The music industry serves as a case in point. While we celebrate the tales of overnight sensations, countless equally gifted musicians toil in obscurity. Often, it isn't merely exceptional talent or artistry that elevates a song to prominence but rather its alignment with cultural trends or its placement in a popular film or television series. For instance, the viral success of "The Macarena" was less about its musical brilliance and more about its perfect timing and catchy dance, illustrating the significant role of luck and timing in achieving success.

Visual arts offer another compelling example through the story of Vincent van Gogh. His genius was not diminished during his lifetime, yet it took a confluence of shifting societal tastes, astute art dealers, and a hefty dose of posthumous luck for his work to be acknowledged as masterpieces.

Now, some might raise a valid point: "What about hard work and perseverance?" Absolutely, hard work is indispensable. Yet, it's essential to recognize that luck favors the prepared. Consider luck as a bus that intermittently arrives. If you're unprepared when it pulls up, you may miss your opportunity. Thus, dedication and relentless practice are crucial; they ensure that when luck does present itself, you're ready to seize it.

Take LeBron James, for example. His extraordinary talent and tireless work ethic are undeniably factors in his success. However, his fortunate combination of physical attributes, the era he was born into, and the right exposure to scouts at a critical juncture also played a significant role. Similarly, J.K. Rowling's perseverance through a barrage of rejections is commendable, but it was luck that ensured her manuscript found its way to the right editor at the right moment.

Interestingly, once an individual secures that initial stroke of luck, a phenomenon called "cumulative advantage" or the "Matthew Effect" takes hold. This principle suggests that success breeds further success. When an artist or athlete gains recognition, they are afforded better opportunities, leading to a compounding effect that widens the gap between those who succeed and those who do not. This cycle can swiftly transform a modest advantage into a chasm separating the "haves" from the "have-nots."

But herein lies the conundrum: our fascination with success stories often blinds us to the countless equally talented individuals who were not afforded that crucial break. We tend to focus on the one-in-a-million successes while neglecting the multitude that didn't enjoy similar fortune. This is a classic case of survivorship bias, where we become enamored with the successful and forget the many who were equally deserving but simply didn't catch the lucky break.

This reality carries significant implications for aspiring artists and athletes, as well as society at large. Lastly, let's address the flipside of luck: misfortune. Just as fortuitous events can propel one to stardom, ill-timed misfortunes can derail even the most promising careers. A sudden injury, a misinterpreted statement, or a shift in public sentiment can swiftly alter the trajectory of a career. The case of Bo Jackson serves as a poignant reminder; despite his unparalleled talent, a freak injury curtailed his athletic journey, underscoring how fickle fortune can be.

Chapter 3.3: Critique and Counter-arguments

- Evaluating studies that downplay luck

The Central Dichotomy: At first glance, the debate over luck versus skill seems straightforward. Society often lauds hard work and talent, framing them as the cornerstones of success. Yet, upon closer examination, it becomes evident that luck plays a far more pivotal role than many are willing to acknowledge. This realization can be jarring, akin to disillusionment about cherished beliefs—think of it as the adult version of discovering that Santa Claus is not real.

Research supports this notion, with studies revealing that random chance can significantly influence outcomes, sometimes overshadowing the contributions of skill and effort. For instance, a mathematical model developed by Italian researchers demonstrated that luck is a more substantial factor in achieving extreme success than IQ or talent. This finding underscores that the most successful individuals in their simulations were often those who experienced the most favorable random events, not necessarily those with superior skills or intellect.

In recognizing the role of luck in success, we must question the validity of naive meritocracy, which posits that success is always a direct reflection of competence. This perspective can inadvertently perpetuate inequality by ignoring how random circumstances can skew perceived merit. If we genuinely seek a society that rewards talent and hard work, we must actively work to mitigate the impact of arbitrary factors that influence success.

To address these disparities, we must consider systemic approaches that level the playing field. Enhancing access to quality education, healthcare, and robust social safety nets are critical steps towards ensuring that meritocracy functions as intended. By providing equitable opportunities, we can better align outcomes with genuine skill and effort rather than with the luck of the draw.

The takeaway from this exploration is not to resign ourselves to fate but rather to embrace a dual strategy of hard work and openness to serendipity. We should strive to refine our skills while remaining vigilant to the opportunities that luck may present. Recognizing that success is a confluence of these elements invites a more nuanced dialogue about fairness, opportunity, and the human experience.

- Common methodological flaws and biases

Diving into the quagmire of research biases and methodological flaws reveals a tangled mess that obscures our understanding of success, meritocracy, and societal fairness. At the heart of this discussion lies the concept of hindsight bias, which, as pointed out by Paul Lazarsfeld, leads us to construct narratives that retroactively glorify our predictive capabilities. This cognitive trap not only misrepresents past events but also distorts our current understanding of success narratives, making us believe that outcomes were inevitable rather than contingent upon a myriad of unpredictable variables.

Consider the analogy of the armchair quarterback who confidently declares they knew the winning play all along. This reflects a larger societal tendency to oversimplify complex realities into digestible success stories. We often latch onto narratives that highlight individual merit while conveniently sidestepping the multitude of factors that contribute to success, including luck. Herein lies a critical flaw: our narratives about achievement are frequently constructed through a lens that minimizes the role of chance. This narrative construction fosters an illusion of meritocracy, where hard work is positioned as the sole determinant of success, despite the reality that systemic barriers and serendipitous events play substantial roles.

The myth of meritocracy is reinforced by our educational institutions, which increasingly demand extraordinary achievements from students. This arms race of credentials not only perpetuates inequalities but also heightens pressures on individuals to conform to unrealistic standards of success. The result? A generation of students grappling with anxiety and disillusionment, believing their worth is tied to their achievements. This situation is exacerbated by the rigidity of our definitions of success, which often ignore the fluidity of opportunity and the inherent randomness of life.

Now, let's introduce luck into this equation. It's a four-letter word that successful individuals often overlook, preferring instead to attribute their accomplishments solely to hard work and perseverance. However, when we scrutinize these success stories, we find that they frequently gloss over the fortuitous circumstances that facilitated those achievements. Much like lottery winners who claim to have a "system," successful people often construct narratives that obscure the randomness inherent in their journeys.

This tendency to downplay luck not only skews our understanding of success but also shapes societal attitudes toward those who struggle. By failing to acknowledge the role of chance, we risk blaming individuals for their misfortunes, perpetuating stigma around poverty or lack of success. Imagine if we were to swap the circumstances of a self-made millionaire with someone living in poverty. The narrative of hard work leading to success would crumble under the weight of reality, revealing the cracks in our societal beliefs about merit and fairness.

In light of these insights, what might a more equitable system look like? One radical proposal is to introduce elements of randomness into selection processes for schools, jobs, and even prestigious speaking engagements. While this idea may initially seem ludicrous, it could serve as a corrective to the illusion of control and fairness that permeates our current frameworks. By recognizing that merit alone does not guarantee success, we could alleviate some pressure from individuals and create a more compassionate society that allows for diverse pathways to achievement.

Yet, why is this proposal not gaining traction? The answer lies in our instinct for narrative coherence. We crave stories that make sense and reinforce our beliefs about hard work leading to success. Challenging this narrative forces us to confront the uncomfortable reality that success is a complex interplay of effort, opportunity, and sheer luck. Until we grapple with this complexity, we will continue to perpetuate a system that is not only inequitable but also detrimental to the well-being of individuals who strive within it.

- Balancing statistical insights with anecdotal evidence

Let's first acknowledge the inherent nature of human cognition: we are, fundamentally, storytellers. This proclivity for narrative shapes our perceptions and interpretations of the world around us. Yet, while anecdotes can engage and resonate, they can also lead us astray when grappling with complex phenomena. This duality is where our exploration begins.

Statistics offer a rigorous framework for understanding trends and patterns, yet they often lack the emotional connection that personal stories provide. For instance, in discussing economic issues, we are bombarded with numbers like GDP growth and unemployment rates, which can feel detached from the real lives they impact. Anecdotal evidence, on the other hand, humanizes these statistics, bringing to light individual experiences that statistics may overlook. However, relying solely on personal narratives can result in misleading generalizations, as they may not accurately represent broader trends.

To navigate this tension, we must strive for a synthesis of both approaches. Just as Joe DiMaggio's legendary hitting streak illustrates a compelling story, it simultaneously highlights the statistical phenomenon known as the "paradox of skill." This paradox posits that as skill levels increase, the role of luck becomes more pronounced in determining outcomes. Thus, while DiMaggio's achievements may inspire awe, they also invite skepticism when viewed through a statistical lens. This interplay between narrative and data underscores the need for a nuanced understanding of events.

One crucial element in this endeavor is context. Statistics devoid of context lack meaning, and anecdotes without situational grounding can lead to misguided conclusions. Therefore, we must actively seek to integrate both forms of evidence, understanding how individual experiences fit within larger frameworks. This requires humility and openness to the idea that our personal anecdotes, while impactful, may not universally apply.

Moreover, our approach to anecdotal evidence should evolve. Instead of treating personal experiences as definitive proof of general truths, we can consider them as data points that warrant further investigation. As we forge this path, we must also be willing to confront challenges. The temptation to oversimplify complex narratives can be strong, leading to binary thinking where issues are painted in stark black and white. We must resist this urge and embrace the multifaceted nature of reality. It's essential to recognize that the world is not only a collection of stories or statistics but a rich tapestry woven from both.

Chapter 4: The Lottery of Birth

Chapter 4.1: Sociological Studies on Birth and Success

- Key research findings on birth circumstances and life outcomes

Let's embark on an exploration of how sociological research illuminates the profound impact of birth circumstances on life outcomes, fundamentally challenging traditional notions of success and emphasizing the role of luck.

At the heart of the discussion lies the often-cited adage, "pull yourself up by your bootstraps," which implies that success is solely the result of individual effort. However, this notion is increasingly critiqued as overly simplistic. Research indicates that the circumstances into which one is born—such as socioeconomic status, family background, and access to resources—play a significant role in shaping life trajectories, often overshadowing personal determination and talent. This perspective underscores a critical realization: luck, defined as the random distribution of advantages and disadvantages at birth, is a major determinant of success and opportunity in life.

Skeptics may argue that emphasizing luck undermines personal accountability and the value of hard work. However, acknowledging the role of luck does not negate the importance of effort. Rather, it encourages a more nuanced understanding of success. Success stories often intertwine talent and hard work with moments of serendipity; recognizing this complexity fosters empathy towards those facing systemic barriers that are not simply overcome by grit alone.

As we reflect on these insights, it becomes imperative to examine our privileges and the societal structures that shape our opportunities. For those who have experienced success, it is vital to consider how much of that success is attributable to individual effort versus inherited advantages. Conversely, for those grappling with adversity, it is essential to acknowledge that external factors may significantly influence their struggles.

Ultimately, this sociological research compels us to rethink success as an intricate tapestry woven from threads of luck, circumstance, and individual agency. By fostering environments rich in opportunities—through equitable education, accessible resources, and supportive networks—we can enhance the chances of success for all individuals, regardless of their starting point.

- The influence of family wealth, education, and social capital

The assertion that hard work alone guarantees success is a deeply ingrained belief in many cultures, particularly within the framework of the American Dream. However, this perspective oversimplifies the complexities of success, often ignoring the profound roles that luck and privilege play in shaping individual outcomes.

To understand the dynamics of success, one must first acknowledge the significance of one's circumstances at birth. Being born into a wealthy family typically comes with advantages—access to quality education, comprehensive healthcare, and influential social networks. Conversely, individuals born into poverty face systemic barriers that can inhibit their potential from the outset. This stark contrast can be likened to competing in a race where some participants begin with a considerable head start, while others are burdened by obstacles that hinder their progress.

Education is a critical arena where privilege manifests. Wealthier families can often afford to place their children in esteemed school districts or private institutions, replete with resources that enhance learning experiences. In contrast, children from less privileged backgrounds frequently attend underfunded schools plagued by overcrowded classrooms and inadequate materials. This disparity in educational quality significantly contributes to the long-term trajectory of students, ultimately affecting their employment opportunities and income potential.

Moreover, the expectations set within families regarding higher education can differ drastically. In affluent households, attending college is often seen as an inevitable step, supported by an established framework that promotes academic achievement. In contrast, students from less affluent backgrounds may perceive higher education as a distant dream, further limiting their aspirations and outcomes.

Social capital, the network of relationships that individuals can draw upon, plays a pivotal role in facilitating opportunities. Those from well-connected families often benefit from introductions to influential figures in various industries, increasing their chances of securing internships and job placements. This reality underscores the adage, "It's not what you know, but who you know." Without access to such networks, individuals from marginalized backgrounds may struggle to find the same opportunities to showcase their talents.

Acknowledging the roles of luck and privilege is crucial for fostering a more equitable society. To begin addressing these disparities, several actionable steps can be taken:

Enhancing Educational Opportunities: Investing in education in underprivileged areas is paramount. This could involve increasing funding for schools, providing access to technology, and creating after-school programs that offer tutoring and mentorship.

Expanding Networks: Initiatives that facilitate networking opportunities for marginalized youth can bridge the gap in social capital. Programs that connect students with mentors in their fields of interest can help create pathways to internships and job opportunities.

Policy Interventions: Implementing policies aimed at reducing income inequality and providing support for low-income families can help dismantle the cycle of poverty. This might include affordable housing initiatives, healthcare access, and childcare support, thereby alleviating some of the burdens that hinder success.

Cultural Shift: A fundamental change in societal attitudes towards success is necessary. Shifting the narrative from the glorification of the "self-made" individual to a recognition of the systemic factors at play can foster greater compassion and understanding for those facing challenges.

Chapter 4.2: Socio-economic Factors and Opportunities

- The impact of geographical location on access to resources

The exploration of geographical location as a determinant of access to resources and opportunities reveals a hilarious landscape shaped by an interplay of socio-economic conditions, cultural influences, and even luck. Geographical location is not merely a backdrop; it is an active player in the distribution of resources that can profoundly shape individual success. This chapter seeks to unravel how the environment in which one resides can dictate not only the availability of essential resources but also the pathways available for success.

A crucial aspect examined is the correlation between geographical location and the availability of resources, which is underscored by the significance of a stimulating environment. Regions that offer abundant educational opportunities, effective training programs, and strategic resource distribution tend to foster innovation and collective progress. In contrast, areas burdened by socio-economic challenges may stifle these opportunities, thereby constraining individual potential. This disparity creates a clear divide; individuals in affluent regions are often positioned to benefit from better resources, enhancing their likelihood of success compared to those in less favorable locations.

Through simulations, researchers have illustrated the stark differences in outcomes based on environmental stimulation. When contrasting regions rich in opportunities with those that are not, it becomes evident that the former consistently produces a higher number of successful individuals. This finding raises critical questions about the inherent advantages conferred by geographical circumstances and challenges the notion that success is solely a product of personal effort and talent.

The geographical context also highlights the disparities faced by individuals in less developed countries, where limited resources can severely restrict opportunities, trapping many in cycles of poverty. In contrast, individuals born into affluent families are often afforded greater opportunities merely due to their geographical location and the resources that accompany it. This inequity raises critical questions about the fairness of success being contingent on one's birthplace rather than individual merit.

Additionally, social and cultural factors intertwine with geographical influences, further complicating access to resources. In certain regions, specific industries may dominate the economic landscape, creating a concentration of opportunities in those fields while neglecting others. Access to quality education and healthcare also varies widely by geographical location, shaping an individual's ability to leverage their talents effectively and achieve their aspirations.

In conclusion, the intricate relationship between geographical location, resources, and opportunities reveals a multifaceted issue that extends beyond mere economic factors. While policies aimed at enhancing resource distribution can yield positive outcomes, the influences of socio-economic conditions, and cultural factors are equally significant. This understanding is vital for addressing systemic inequalities and creating a future where success is determined not by geographical happenstance but by individual potential and effort.

- Education and its role in leveling the playing field

Education serves as a powerful tool for leveling the playing field and fostering equal opportunities for individuals from varied backgrounds. One significant aspect highlighted is that a strong educational foundation can enhance an individual's chances of success. It is posited that policies aimed at improving educational access can lead to greater societal progress and innovation, suggesting that education acts as a catalyst for social mobility, enabling individuals to surmount barriers and reach their full potential.

Moreover, a provocative notion regarding the college admissions process, job offers, and conference invitations, proposing a lottery system to select candidates. This idea aims to dismantle biases and create a more transparent and equitable selection process. While it may not entirely eradicate injustice, it challenges the prevailing systems and underscores the necessity for a more honest approach. This perspective invites critical contemplation on how traditional methods can perpetuate inequality and suggests innovative alternatives to foster fairness.

Education transcends mere knowledge acquisition; it cultivates critical thinking, creativity, and problem-solving abilities essential for navigating the complexities of contemporary life. It empowers individuals to make informed decisions and enhances social cohesion by exposing them to diverse perspectives and cultures. This multifaceted development is crucial in a world that increasingly values adaptability and collaboration.

We also need to challenge conventional metrics of success, arguing that it should not be solely defined by academic accomplishments. Instead, we have to advocate for a broader view that recognizes various skills and qualities, thereby allowing individuals from diverse backgrounds to highlight their unique strengths.

Furthermore, education plays a pivotal role in promoting social mobility by equipping individuals with the necessary knowledge and skills to secure improved employment prospects and higher wages. Enhancing access to quality education for everyone, regardless of their socio-economic status, significantly increases the likelihood of breaking the cycle of poverty and achieving upward mobility.

The ability to challenge entrenched attitudes through education is crucial for creating an environment where all individuals feel valued and empowered. Systemic inequalities must be addressed, with equal access to resources and the creation of supportive environments being vital components to empower individuals to thrive.

- Social mobility and its limitations

Social mobility, defined as the capacity for individuals to ascend or descend the social hierarchy, serves as a vital indicator of societal equity and access to opportunities. However, an exploration of the various influences on social mobility reveals a complex interplay of factors that complicate this seemingly straightforward concept. Central to this discussion is the notion of luck, which often goes unrecognized in narratives of success. While individual effort and determination are crucial, the role of serendipity cannot be understated; many who achieve success may fail to acknowledge the favorable circumstances that paved their paths. This oversight perpetuates the myth that social mobility is entirely meritocratic, obscuring the reality that fortunate opportunities often play a pivotal role in elevating one's status.

Delving deeper, it becomes clear that the conditions into which individuals are born significantly shape their prospects for upward mobility. Those from affluent backgrounds typically have access to superior educational resources and networks that facilitate their advancement, creating a stark contrast for individuals raised in disadvantaged environments. The latter group frequently encounters systemic barriers—such as inadequate schooling, limited access to mentorship, and entrenched socioeconomic disparities—that thwart their aspirations. Such inequities illustrate that social mobility is not merely a reflection of personal ambition but is intricately linked to broader social structures and historical contexts.

Moreover, the distribution of opportunities is far from equitable, particularly for individuals in marginalized communities or developing nations. Even when individuals possess remarkable talent and potential, the absence of platforms to showcase and develop these abilities drastically limits their ability to ascend the social ladder. This disparity emphasizes the necessity for systemic reforms aimed at leveling the playing field.

Wealth concentration among a select few creates substantial barriers for the majority, effectively locking them in positions of limited opportunity. Addressing this issue requires a commitment to resource redistribution and the establishment of equitable systems that promote the emergence of talent from diverse backgrounds. It is imperative to recognize that social mobility cannot be solely attributed to individual efforts; rather, it demands a critical examination of the structural impediments that exist within society.

Unfavorable circumstances, such as economic hardships or health crises, can derail even the most diligent individuals from achieving upward mobility.

Chapter 4.3: Personal Stories from Different Backgrounds

- The role of mentorship and support networks

Mentorship and support networks are fundamental pillars that underpin personal and professional growth, shaping the trajectories of individuals striving for success. A critical examination of these dynamics reveals that success seldom occurs in isolation; instead, it is often the product of relationships cultivated through mentorship and supportive communities. The notion of self-made success is frequently romanticized, yet a closer look uncovers a tapestry of interconnected individuals who contribute to each other's journeys, highlighting that achievement is inherently collaborative.

Mentorship plays a pivotal role in this ecosystem, serving as a beacon of guidance for those navigating the complexities of their careers and personal aspirations. Mentors, equipped with the wisdom borne from their own experiences, provide invaluable insights that can steer mentees away from common pitfalls while promoting informed decision-making. This mentorship relationship creates a safe haven where individuals can articulate their goals, confront their challenges, and cultivate the skills necessary for success. The significance of mentorship is underscored by the observation that understanding the codes and values of the communities one wishes to enter is crucial; mentors can impart this knowledge, thereby enhancing the mentees' ability to create value within their respective fields.

Support networks extend the benefits of mentorship, encompassing a broader community of individuals who collectively foster an environment of encouragement and resource-sharing. These networks may manifest as professional organizations, alumni associations, or informal gatherings among peers. They not only provide a sense of belonging but also stimulate collaboration and the exchange of ideas, which are vital for personal and professional development. By being part of such networks, individuals can leverage the collective strength of their community to overcome challenges and pursue opportunities more effectively.

The importance of diversity within mentorship and support networks cannot be overstated. Engaging with a variety of mentors from different backgrounds and experiences enriches the learning process, exposing individuals to new perspectives and challenging preconceived notions. This diversity encourages critical thinking and fosters a comprehensive approach to problem-solving, which is essential in today's multifaceted professional landscape. The broader the spectrum of voices one encounters, the more nuanced their understanding of the world becomes, ultimately enhancing their capacity for innovation and adaptability.

Moreover, the reciprocal nature of mentorship and support networks enriches the experiences of both mentors and mentees. Mentors are not just conduits of knowledge; they also experience personal growth and fulfillment through their engagements with mentees. This interaction allows them to reflect on their journeys and reinforce their own understanding while contributing to the cultivation of future leaders. Similarly, those within support networks find satisfaction in uplifting others, creating a cycle of mutual support that perpetuates growth and success.

- Overcoming systemic barriers and leveraging opportunities

Overcoming systemic barriers and leveraging opportunities is a complex endeavor that requires individuals to adopt a holistic approach, blending advocacy, recognition of external factors like luck, proactive behavior, and the pursuit of mentorship and support networks. These elements interact in a way that can either facilitate or hinder personal and collective progress.

At the forefront of this journey is the necessity to advocate for policies that create equitable opportunities. As outlined previously, a stimulating environment enriched with education, training, and resource distribution is crucial for collective innovation and success. Engaging in advocacy means not only voicing concerns but also actively participating in initiatives that aim to dismantle systemic inequities. Individuals can contribute to this cause by joining advocacy groups and participating in community initiatives that promote access to quality education and fair distribution of resources. This engagement is not merely beneficial for the individual but fosters a more just society that uplifts everyone.

However, while advocacy is essential, it is equally important to recognize the role of luck in the equation of success. This recognition fosters empathy for those who, despite their diligence, do not achieve similar results due to circumstances beyond their control. In addition, individuals must adopt a proactive mindset to enhance their chances of success. By cultivating habits such as setting clear goals, prioritizing effectively, and fostering positive relationships, individuals can create an environment conducive to attracting opportunities.

Stepping outside of one's comfort zone and embracing new experiences can lead to serendipitous encounters that facilitate personal and professional growth. Networking and seeking out new experiences can serve as gateways to unexpected opportunities, reinforcing the idea that action breeds luck. By remaining open to change and willing to explore novel avenues, individuals can significantly expand their prospects.

Chapter 5: Redefining Success: Beyond Personal Control

Chapter 5.1: Philosophical Perspectives on Success

- Various philosophical views on success and luck

The exploration of diverse philosophical perspectives regarding the roles of luck and talent in success reveals a rich tapestry that challenges traditional notions of achievement and merit. Seneca, the ancient Roman philosopher, asserts a staunch belief in the supremacy of individual effort, famously claiming that "luck does not exist." This perspective aligns with a naive meritocracy, where success is viewed as a direct consequence of one's abilities and hard work, disregarding the myriad external factors that can influence outcomes. This rigid stance can lead to a dismissal of the complexities of human experience.

In contrast, Nicolo Machiavelli, writing during the Italian Renaissance, introduces a more nuanced view, acknowledging that "luck is the arbiter of half of our actions." This recognition of chance as a significant determinant in the course of our lives invites a more balanced understanding of success, where individual talent and effort remain vital, but are complemented by the capricious nature of fortune. Such a perspective encourages a more realistic appraisal of personal achievements, suggesting that success cannot solely be attributed to individual merit without considering the influence of external circumstances.

Building on these philosophical foundations, Nassim Nicholas Taleb, a contemporary statistician, provocatively argues that "lack matters more than talent." This assertion has ignited widespread debate, as it challenges prevailing attitudes that prioritize hard work and skill over the unpredictable elements of luck. Taleb's position gains empirical support from the research conducted by Italian physicists Pluchino and Raspisarda, alongside economist Biondo, who developed a mathematical model highlighting the overwhelming role of luck in career trajectories.

- Moral and ethical considerations in attributing success

In examining John Rawls' concept of the "veil of ignorance," we uncover a transformative approach to reconciling liberty and equality within the framework of a just society. The veil of ignorance serves as a philosophical instrument that encourages individuals to design societal rules without any preconceived notions regarding their personal circumstances. By inviting participants to imagine the establishment of societal norms without knowledge of their own age, gender, race, socioeconomic status, or abilities, this concept effectively dismantles personal biases and interests. As a result, it fosters a more equitable perspective that is sensitive to the needs of all individuals, particularly those who are most disadvantaged.

The implications of employing the veil of ignorance in societal design are significant. Individuals who engage with this framework are compelled to prioritize fairness and equality, recognizing that any person could occupy any social position. Within this context, Rawls articulates two foundational principles of justice that emerge from such deliberations. The first principle asserts that every individual deserves equal basic liberties, ensuring that each person can enjoy the most comprehensive freedoms possible, provided these do not infringe upon the freedoms of others. The second principle, referred to as the difference principle, posits that social and economic inequalities must be structured in a manner that benefits the least advantaged members of society.

Moreover, the veil of ignorance acts as a catalyst for rational decision-making. When individuals are stripped of their specific identities and remain unaware of their future societal positions, they are naturally incentivized to create a system that is inherently just and equitable. The relevance of this concept is particularly pronounced in contemporary policy discussions, where it challenges policymakers to transcend their personal biases and consider the broader implications of their choices on vulnerable populations.

However, it is important to acknowledge that the veil of ignorance is not without its criticisms. Detractors often raise concerns about the feasibility of applying such an abstract concept to real-world decision-making, questioning whether individuals can genuinely detach from their identities and inherent interests during the deliberative process. Additionally, some argue that the veil may overlook the complexities of cultural identity, highlighting the necessity for diverse perspectives to truly achieve justice.

By nurturing an environment conducive to equitable principles, the veil of ignorance remains an essential tool for addressing societal disparities, while simultaneously inviting ongoing dialogue about its practical applications and cultural considerations. This dynamic interplay enriches our understanding of justice and reinforces the commitment to fostering a society that honors both liberty and equality.

Chapter 5.2: Techniques for Acknowledging Luck

Cultivating awareness of luck in one's life can significantly enhance personal growth and resilience, as it encourages individuals to recognize the multitude of factors that contribute to their experiences. Engaging in mindfulness exercises serves as a foundational practice, allowing individuals to reflect daily on fortunate events that might otherwise go unnoticed.

This intentional reflection can help individuals acknowledge moments of serendipity, fostering a deeper appreciation for the seemingly random occurrences that shape their lives. Furthermore, gratitude journaling complements this practice by providing a structured approach to recording and celebrating experiences of luck and favorable outcomes. By regularly writing down instances where they feel fortunate, individuals reinforce positive thinking patterns and cultivate a sense of abundance, which can be transformative in their overall outlook on life.

In addition to these reflective practices, participating in random acts of kindness can illuminate the interconnectedness of luck. When individuals give to others, they not only spread goodwill but also experience a reciprocal sense of fortune through the joy of making a difference in someone else's life. This exchange highlights the notion that luck is not solely a solitary experience; instead, it is often intertwined with the actions and kindness of others. Sharing stories of personal experiences related to luck further enriches this understanding, as discussing these moments with others can reinforce awareness and create a community of shared experiences.

Moreover, cultivating humility is crucial in recognizing the contributions of others to one's achievements. By emphasizing the role that external support and lucky events play in personal success, individuals can develop a more balanced perspective on their accomplishments. Expressing gratitude towards those who have influenced or supported one's journey is an essential practice that fosters deeper connections and acknowledges the collaborative nature of success.

Reflecting on personal journeys with an open mind also invites individuals to embrace vulnerability. By examining both failures and unexpected successes, they can gain insights into how luck has shaped their paths and decisions. This reflection not only promotes self-awareness but also encourages people to learn from their experiences, ultimately motivating them to adopt a growth mindset. By viewing luck as a catalyst for future growth, individuals can build resilience.

Chapter 6: Fostering a Compassionate Society

Chapter 6.1: Policy Recommendations for Fairness

- Suggested policies to reduce inequality and enhance opportunities

We cannot simply throw up our hands in despair. No, as responsible stewards of society, we must roll up our sleeves and get to work crafting policies that can meaningfully address these entrenched inequities. And I believe the key lies in embracing a radical shift in our approach to resource distribution.

The evidence is clear: concentrating resources and rewards in the hands of a select few is a recipe for perpetuating the Matthew effect, where the rich get richer and the poor get poorer. Instead, we must explore innovative ways to periodically redistribute funds and opportunities in a more egalitarian manner.

One shining example of this approach can be found in the Danish Council for Independent Research. Recognizing the limitations of their existing funding model, they implemented a "Sapere Aude" program that dedicates a portion of their budget to a random selection process. The results have been nothing short of remarkable. By giving a chance to those who may have been overlooked by the traditional system, the Sapere Aude program has unearthed a treasure trove of innovative and impactful research projects that have had a tangible effect on the lives of citizens.

But the Danes are not alone in their quest for a more equitable distribution of resources. In Germany, the Deutsche Forschungsgemeinschaft (DFG) has also embraced the power of randomness, setting aside a portion of their funding for a lottery-based allocation system. And the results have been equally impressive, with the DFG's "Experiment!" program uncovering a wealth of novel and transformative ideas that may have otherwise been left in the shadows.

In New Zealand, for instance, the Marsden Fund has set aside a portion of its budget for a "Catalyst" program that specifically targets high-risk, high-reward research projects. By embracing the power of serendipity, this program has uncovered a treasure trove of innovative breakthroughs that may have otherwise been overlooked by the traditional funding landscape.

Similarly, in the United Kingdom, the Engineering and Physical Sciences Research Council (EPSRC) has implemented a "Responsive Mode" funding scheme that allocates a significant portion of its budget to unsolicited research proposals. The rationale behind this approach is simple: by creating more opportunities for the "average-successful" to thrive, we can unlock a wellspring of untapped human potential that has long been overlooked.

We would do well to take a page from the playbook of these trailblazing institutions. Imagine if college admissions, job offers at tech companies, and even TED talk invitations were determined by a similar lottery system. Granted, this may seem like a radical departure from the status quo, but it has the potential to puncture the "pressure balloon" that has become the modern education and career landscape.

Of course, I can already hear the objections: "But what about merit? Shouldn't the most qualified individuals be the ones to succeed?" To which I would respond: merit, while important, is far from the sole determinant of an individual's potential to thrive and contribute to society. Oftentimes, it is the serendipitous confluence of opportunity, environment, and innate talent that truly unlocks an individual's ability to flourish.

This is where a progressive tax scheme comes into play. By ensuring that those who have reaped the greatest rewards from society's bounty also contribute the most back to the system, we can create a virtuous cycle of reinvestment and shared prosperity. The logic is simple: if we have been able to exploit the opportunities available to us and amass significant wealth, then we have a moral obligation to "pay it forward" and support the development of the next generation.

Take, for instance, the Nordic countries, where progressive taxation has been a cornerstone of their social welfare policies for decades. In Sweden, for example, the top marginal tax rate can reach as high as 57%, with the revenue generated from these taxes being funneled into robust social safety nets, world-class education systems, and cutting-edge infrastructure projects. The result? A society that boasts some of the highest levels of social mobility, economic opportunity, and overall well-being in the world.

This is not about punishing success, but rather recognizing that true progress can only be achieved when we all have a vested interest in the collective well-being of our communities. By embracing a more progressive tax structure, we can fund crucial investments in education, infrastructure, and social services - the very foundations that enable individuals, regardless of their starting point, to reach their full potential.

It is a lofty goal, to be sure, but one that is well within our grasp. All it takes is the courage to challenge the status quo and the vision to reimagine the very foundations of our social and economic systems. And with the inspiring examples of success that we have at our fingertips, I have no doubt that we are up to the task.

Chapter 6.2: Empathy in Social and Economic Policies

- The benefits of empathy-driven policy making

Empathy in social and economic policymaking is not merely an idealistic notion; it is a fundamental necessity for creating effective governance that genuinely addresses the diverse needs and challenges faced by individuals and communities. The disconnect between policymakers and the lived realities of the populations is mindblowing, they are a significant barrier to meaningful change. Often, decisions are made based on quantitative data, which overlooks the qualitative aspects of human experience. This reliance on metrics can lead to policies that, while efficient in theory, are ineffective in practice because they fail to consider the human element at the core of social issues.

It is crucial to understand that the context surrounding individuals' lives influences their opportunities and outcomes. A purely meritocratic system may not only perpetuate inequality but can exacerbate the wealth gap. An empathetic approach would recognize that not all individuals start from the same place; systemic barriers, such as lack of access to education, discrimination, or socioeconomic disadvantages, significantly affect their ability to succeed. Policies that aim to level the playing field must be informed by an understanding of these challenges, providing targeted support for those who need it most.

Consider the example of government grant programs. An empathetic policymaking approach would not simply reward those who have already demonstrated success but would actively seek out and support individuals with untapped potential from diverse backgrounds. By identifying and nurturing these promising individuals, we can create a system that not only encourages social mobility but also harnesses a broader range of talents and perspectives. This unlocking of human potential can lead to increased innovation and societal advancement.

The healthcare sector also presents a fertile ground for the application of empathy in policymaking. A healthcare system designed with empathy would seek to understand the unique barriers individuals face in accessing care, whether those barriers are financial, cultural, or geographical. By tailoring policies to address these specific needs, we can create a more equitable healthcare system that promotes holistic well-being rather than merely treating illness. This empathetic approach can lead to improved health outcomes and a more resilient healthcare infrastructure, ultimately benefiting society as a whole.

In education, an empathetic perspective is equally vital. Recognizing that students come from varied backgrounds and possess unique learning styles is crucial in developing effective educational programs. A school system that nurtures not only academic excellence but also the social and emotional well-being of its students can foster critical thinking, creativity, and a sense of purpose. Such an approach prepares young people to navigate the complexities of modern life and empowers them to contribute positively to their communities.

Moreover, the implications of empathy-driven policymaking extend into urban planning, environmental protection, and criminal justice. Each domain requires a nuanced understanding of the experiences of the people affected by these policies. By incorporating empathy into these areas, policymakers can create solutions that resonate more deeply with community members and address their real-world needs.

However, the transition to an empathy-centered approach in governance is not without its challenges. It necessitates a fundamental shift away from technocratic, top-down models toward collaborative, bottom-up strategies. This shift includes investing in research that captures the qualitative experiences of individuals and communities, fostering a culture of empathy within institutions, and ensuring that policymakers are not only skilled but also deeply connected to the human aspects of their work.

- Examples of empathetic leadership and its impact

Empathetic leadership serves as a catalyst for driving positive social and economic change across various sectors by fostering environments that prioritize understanding and collaboration. Taking cues from leaders like Jacqueline Novogratz, the founder of Acumen, we can see how this method transcends traditional top-down leadership models. Novogratz's emphasis on listening to the communities she serves allows for the empowerment of local entrepreneurs, leading to solutions that are not only innovative but also deeply rooted in the context of the communities they aim to benefit.

For instance, Acumen's investment in Sanergy, which revolutionizes sanitation in Nairobi's slums, exemplifies this empathetic approach. Rather than imposing a centralized waste management system that wouldn't suit the densely populated areas, Sanergy's founders developed a decentralized network of community-owned toilets. This not only addresses the immediate need for sanitation but also instills a sense of ownership and dignity among the users. By prioritizing community input and needs, empathetic leadership can tackle root causes rather than merely treating symptoms, as evidenced by the successes achieved by organizations like the Harlem Children's Zone, which provides comprehensive support to children and families to break the cycle of poverty.

Furthermore, the business sector is witnessing a shift towards empathetic leadership as companies like Patagonia prioritize stakeholder well-being over short-term profits. Under Yvon Chouinard's leadership, Patagonia's commitment to sustainable practices and employee welfare has resulted in a loyal customer base and impressive financial performance. This demonstrates that empathy in leadership not only enhances social responsibility but also contributes to long-term business success.

Moreover, in public policy, empathetic leadership is essential in addressing complex societal challenges. Acumen's investment in the Embrace Infant Warmer showcases the impact of community-driven innovation in global health. By involving local healthcare providers in the design of the device, the solution is not only effective but culturally appropriate, thereby enhancing trust and engagement within the community.

To incorporate empathetic leadership into our own work and lives, individuals can begin by actively listening to the needs and concerns of others. This involves stepping into the shoes of those we aim to support and understanding their context. Additionally, developing a deeper awareness of the codes and values of various communities can enhance our ability to communicate effectively and create value within those contexts.

- Building a culture of compassion in organizations

In an age where traditional metrics of success often prioritize efficiency and profitability over human well-being, it becomes essential to re-evaluate our approaches to organizational dynamics. Compassionate workplaces can be transformative, creating environments where individuals feel valued and supported, ultimately leading to enhanced productivity and innovation.

To truly appreciate the significance of compassion in organizational culture, one must recognize that organizations are not just mechanical entities but are instead vibrant ecosystems composed of individuals with diverse backgrounds, experiences, and aspirations. Each employee contributes to the collective knowledge and capability of the organization, and as such, their well-being should be prioritized. This perspective challenges the predominant view that individual voice and autonomy are the only pathways to success.

Such practices can lead to an environment where employees feel safe to express their opinions and contribute ideas without fear of reprisal, which is crucial for fostering innovation. For example, Patagonia exemplifies this approach by prioritizing employee welfare through generous benefits and support systems, which in turn cultivates loyalty and high employee satisfaction.

Moreover, the integration of compassion should extend beyond leadership to the organizational fabric itself. This means embedding compassionate practices into recruitment, onboarding, and employee development processes. Organizations can achieve this by implementing training programs that emphasize emotional intelligence and interpersonal skills, equipping employees at all levels with the tools necessary to foster a supportive workplace culture.

In the corporate realm, leaders like Satya Nadella at Microsoft have begun to challenge the traditional profit-centric model, advocating instead for a purpose-driven approach that prioritizes empathy and collaboration. Nadella's emphasis on understanding customer and community needs has led to innovations that align with social responsibility, showcasing how compassion can drive both organizational success and broader societal benefits. This shift in perspective allows organizations to view themselves as integral parts of the communities they serve, expanding their impact beyond mere profitability.

Critics may argue that fostering a culture of compassion could hinder performance or competitiveness. However, evidence suggests that organizations that prioritize employee well-being not only retain talent but also enjoy superior financial performance. The argument here is that compassion does not detract from productivity; rather, it enhances it by creating a motivated and engaged workforce capable of driving innovation and change. The challenge lies in shifting mindsets from seeing compassion as a liability to recognizing it as a strategic asset.

Chapter 6.3: Success Stories of Compassionate Policies

- Programs that have successfully integrated empathy and fairness

The quest for success and progress in society hinges on our collective ability to cultivate an environment that prioritizes empathy-driven policies and programs.

At the heart of this discussion is the understanding that success is not purely a product of individual effort or merit. Instead, it results from a complex interplay of factors.

The Stockton Economic Empowerment Demonstration (SEED) highlights the transformative potential of unconditional financial support. By providing a monthly stipend to selected residents, SEED not only alleviates immediate financial strain but also fosters a sense of agency among recipients. The positive outcomes reported—ranging from improved mental health to greater financial stability—demonstrate how a compassionate approach can yield substantial benefits for both individuals and the broader community. The rejection of the "deserving versus undeserving poor" narrative within this program further emphasizes the inherent dignity of all individuals, regardless of their circumstances. This perspective is crucial in reframing societal attitudes toward poverty and economic disparity.

Implementing empathy-driven policies, however, is fraught with challenges. Policymakers and leaders must navigate a landscape often dominated by entrenched beliefs in meritocracy and individualism. Resistance arises from those who view such initiatives as undermining personal responsibility. Yet, as we have seen through the examples of HCZ and SEED, the long-term benefits of fostering a more equitable society far outweigh the short-term discomfort associated with challenging existing paradigms. The rewards extend beyond the immediate beneficiaries; communities as a whole thrive when their most vulnerable members are supported and uplifted.

In this context, it becomes imperative for aspiring authors, policymakers, and change-makers to harness the power of empathy in their endeavors. By listening to the stories of those who have been marginalized and integrating their experiences into policy development, we can craft solutions that genuinely address the needs of all community members. This requires courage to question the status quo and to champion policies that prioritize collective well-being over individual accolades.

- Lessons learned and recommendations for future initiatives

A critical recommendation for future initiatives is the establishment of robust impact assessments and ongoing evaluations. By systematically measuring outcomes and understanding the unintended consequences of policies, leaders can adapt their strategies to better serve community needs. This data-driven approach not only strengthens the justification for sustained investment but also positions policymakers as responsive and accountable to the communities they aim to uplift.

Sustainable funding is another pillar necessary for the success of impactful initiatives. Many promising programs have faltered due to reliance on unstable political cycles or inconsistent philanthropic support. Exploring innovative financing models, such as public-private partnerships or social impact bonds, can provide the financial stability required to sustain these essential programs over the long term.

Lastly, storytelling and community engagement play a pivotal role in amplifying the voices of those who are too often marginalized. Successful empathy-driven initiatives are those that create platforms for individuals to share their experiences, fostering deeper understanding and inspiring collective action. Such narratives not only humanize the issues but also galvanize public support for policies that prioritize fairness and opportunity for all.

Chapter 7: The Role of Talent and Skill

Chapter 7.1: Differentiating Talent, Skill, and Luck

- Definitions and distinctions between talent, skill, and luck

Talent, often viewed as an innate quality, serves as the foundation upon which skill is built. While talent can predispose an individual toward a particular proficiency, it is the deliberate practice that transforms this potential into skill. Skill, defined as the ability to execute knowledge adeptly, emerges from repeated engagement and refinement, highlighting the importance of sustained effort in any domain.

However, the elusive factor of luck complicates this relationship considerably. Luck, which can be defined as the occurrence of events outside one's control that significantly impact outcomes, introduces an unpredictable element into the equation.

Visualizing the dynamics of talent, skill, and luck can be likened to a continuum. At one extreme lies pure luck—think of games of chance like lotteries—while at the other end rests pure skill, exemplified by chess or athletics, where success is largely determined by an individual's ability and preparation. Yet, most human endeavors occupy a space in between, where a confluence of these elements creates a complex dance, often leading to unexpected results.

This complexity becomes particularly salient in domains such as entrepreneurship, the arts, and academia. In entrepreneurship, an individual armed with talent and skill may still fail to succeed without the fortuitous alignment of market conditions, timing, and connections. Conversely, an entrepreneur lacking in some areas may unexpectedly thrive due to a serendipitous opportunity. Similarly, artists and scientists often find that their recognition hinges not solely on their genius but also on external factors like critical reception or the timing of their work, which underscores the unpredictable nature of success.

As we navigate this intricate landscape, it is crucial to confront our inherent biases. The illusion of control often leads us to overestimate the influence of personal agency while downplaying the role of external factors. Ultimately, the interplay of talent, skill, and luck is a multifaceted phenomenon that encourages us to reflect on our assumptions about success.

- How these factors interplay in achieving success

The complex interplay between talent, skill, and luck in the pursuit of success has long intrigued scholars and practitioners across various domains. Recent research highlights the significant role luck plays in determining success, suggesting that approximately half of the disparities in income and wealth can be attributed to serendipitous circumstances rather than solely to individual effort or talent.

The concept of the "arc of skill" provides a valuable lens through which to view this interplay, particularly in physical pursuits where an individual's journey typically follows a trajectory of growth, peak performance, and eventual decline. This arc is influenced by biological factors, such as muscle composition and aging, yet it is further complicated when we extend our analysis to domains like entrepreneurship, academia, and creative endeavors. Here, the nuances of talent, skill, and luck coalesce into a symphony of factors that can propel or hinder progress.

- Examples highlighting the balance between them

The intricate interplay between talent, skill, and luck is fundamental in shaping an individual's journey toward success, as vividly illustrated by the experiences of figures such as Michael Phelps, the founders of Airbnb, and Vincent van Gogh. In the realm of sports, Michael Phelps stands out as a quintessential example of this dynamic. His extraordinary talent is evident in his physical attributes—long limbs and a flexible body ideal for swimming—which set the stage for his achievements. However, it was his relentless pursuit of skill, demonstrated through rigorous training regimens and meticulous attention to technique, that allowed him to maximize his natural abilities. Yet, despite this formidable combination, Phelps's success was not solely predicated on talent and skill; luck played an influential role as well. The absence of injuries during critical competitions, favorable weather conditions, and even the unforeseen circumstances of his opponents contributed to his remarkable Olympic achievements.

Transitioning to the entrepreneurial landscape, the founders of Airbnb—Brian Chesky, Joe Gebbia, and Nathan Blecharczyk—provide a compelling case study of how the triad of talent, skill, and luck can intertwine to transform an idea into a global phenomenon. Their innate entrepreneurial talent, coupled with a keen understanding of market dynamics, enabled them to identify and capitalize on an unfulfilled demand for alternative lodging during a pivotal moment. Their innovative approach to business, characterized by agility and creativity, was crucial in navigating the early challenges they faced. However, it is essential to acknowledge the serendipitous elements that influenced their trajectory, such as the opportune timing of their launch during the 2008 Democratic National Convention and the chance to participate in a prestigious startup accelerator program, which were pivotal in scaling their business.

In the art world, Vincent van Gogh's story further exemplifies the complex relationship between talent, skill, and luck. Van Gogh's prodigious artistic talent and unique vision were evident in his prolific output, yet his struggle for recognition during his lifetime underscores the often unpredictable nature of success in the arts. Despite his unwavering dedication to honing his craft, which reflects an intense commitment to skill development, van Gogh faced considerable challenges in gaining appreciation for his work. It was posthumously, through the fortunate discovery of his paintings by a new wave of art enthusiasts and shifting cultural trends, that his genius began to be acknowledged and valued, illustrating how external circumstances can dramatically alter one's legacy.

There exists a pervasive tendency to attribute achievements solely to individual effort and merit while downplaying the role of chance encounters and external factors. This "illusion of control" can skew our perspectives.

Chapter 7.2: Case Studies of Balanced Success

- The role of perseverance and passion in their journeys

In the pursuit of balanced success, where talent, skill, and luck converge, two often overlooked yet pivotal factors emerge as the driving forces behind extraordinary achievements: perseverance and passion. These psychological characteristics serve as the bedrock upon which individuals build their journeys towards success, transforming potential into tangible accomplishments. So how do perseverance and passion shape the trajectory of those who achieve balanced success?

Throughout extensive research on the psychological underpinnings of achievement and creativity, I have consistently observed the profound impact of perseverance and passion across diverse fields. These traits transcend the boundaries of innate talent and acquired skill, embodying the unwavering dedication and fervent enthusiasm that individuals bring to their pursuits. Numerous studies and scholarly works have corroborated this observation, highlighting the significance of these characteristics in domains ranging from finance and business to sports, art, music, literature, and science (Duckworth et al., 2007; Vallerand et al., 2003).

Perseverance, often likened to grit in psychological literature, manifests as the ability to persist in the face of challenges, setbacks, and failures. It is the unwavering determination to continue striving, even when the path ahead seems fraught with obstacles or shrouded in uncertainty. Without this tenacity, even the most prodigious talent and refined skill can wither, as individuals may succumb to the temptation of surrender when confronted with adversity. However, when perseverance is coupled with talent and skill, it becomes a formidable force, enabling individuals to surmount challenges, glean wisdom from failures, and ultimately achieve their goals.

Passion, on the other hand, represents the intense enthusiasm and profound love one harbors for their chosen pursuit. It serves as the internal combustion engine that drives individuals to chase their dreams with unwavering dedication and commitment. Passion infuses one's work with a sense of purpose and fulfillment, transforming the journey towards success into an intrinsically rewarding experience. When individuals are passionate about their endeavors, they are more inclined to invest additional effort, push beyond perceived limitations, and continuously refine their skills and knowledge base.

It is crucial to recognize that the significance of perseverance and passion extends beyond the realm of individual success, permeating into the broader web of overall well-being and life satisfaction. When individuals are propelled by their passions and persevere through challenges, they experience a profound sense of fulfillment and personal growth. This alignment with core values and interests fosters a greater likelihood of achieving balance and contentment in their pursuits.

Luck and opportunity, as previously discussed, can play a pivotal role in creating favorable circumstances and opening doors that might otherwise remain closed. However, it is the synergistic combination of talent, skill, luck, perseverance, and passion that ultimately leads to balanced success. How can we nurture these qualities alongside our talents and skills? How might we remain resilient in the face of adversity while maintaining our enthusiasm for our chosen path? By grappling with these questions, we can begin to chart our own course towards balanced success.

Chapter 7.3: Strategies to Enhance Skills and Talents

- Practical tips for skill development and talent nurturing

In exploring the pathways through which individuals can maximize their potential and achieve greater success, it becomes evident that practical strategies play a pivotal role in skill development and talent nurturing. Central to this endeavor is the creation of a stimulating environment, which acts as a fertile ground for growth and innovation. Surrounding oneself with inspiring individuals and engaging in experiences that challenge the norm fosters a mindset open to new ideas and perspectives. This approach not only broadens one's horizons but also enhances the ability to adapt and excel in various situations, echoing the sentiment that a supportive environment is crucial for personal and professional development.

Education stands as a cornerstone in this journey. A commitment to pursuing quality education—be it through formal courses, workshops, or mentorship—equips individuals with essential knowledge and skills. This foundation not only enhances one's capabilities but also lays the groundwork for ongoing growth and adaptation in an ever-evolving landscape. Intensive training further complements educational pursuits. Engaging in focused and deliberate practice is vital for refining skills. The importance of this commitment cannot be overstated; whether through repetition, professional coaching, or self-directed learning, consistent training propels individuals toward mastery in their chosen fields.

Moreover, developing emotional intelligence emerges as a critical factor in navigating the complexities of interpersonal dynamics. Understanding and managing one's emotions, alongside empathizing with others, enhances communication skills and fosters resilient relationships. Such emotional acuity enables individuals to handle challenges gracefully, thereby reinforcing their capacity for success. Equally vital is the cultivation of creative thinking. Embracing innovation and encouraging oneself to explore unconventional ideas can yield unique solutions to problems. Engaging in creative activities stimulates mental agility, allowing individuals to differentiate themselves within their professional domains.

Determination and resilience are indispensable qualities in the pursuit of skill development. The journey is often riddled with setbacks and failures, but viewing these obstacles as learning opportunities is essential. A strong determination to achieve set goals, coupled with a resilient mindset, empowers individuals to navigate adversity and persist in their aspirations. Seeking feedback is also a cornerstone of continuous improvement. Actively soliciting constructive criticism from mentors and peers not only highlights areas for development but also encourages a culture of learning. Staying abreast of industry trends further enhances one's adaptability and relevance in a competitive landscape.

Finally, networking and collaboration serve as powerful avenues for skill enhancement and talent nurturing. Building connections with like-minded individuals fosters a supportive community and opens doors to collaborative projects, enriching the collective knowledge and expertise available to all involved. This shared experience can lead to innovative solutions and exciting opportunities that might otherwise remain out of reach.

- The importance of continuous learning and improvement

Continuous learning and improvement are essential in today's rapidly evolving world, especially regarding skill development and talent nurturing. The relentless pace of technological advancement and shifting methodologies necessitate that individuals adopt a mindset oriented toward lifelong learning. Those who embrace this mindset are not only better equipped to adapt but also to thrive, as they cultivate a robust skill set that remains relevant in a competitive landscape. One of the core reasons for the importance of continuous learning is the need to keep pace with change. As industries evolve, the skills that were once deemed essential may quickly become obsolete. Individuals who engage in continuous learning ensure that they remain abreast of the latest trends and advancements in their respective fields, thereby enhancing their competitiveness and relevance in the job market.

Moreover, continuous learning allows individuals to broaden their skill sets beyond their current expertise, fostering versatility and adaptability. By exploring new disciplines and acquiring diverse skills, individuals position themselves to tackle a wider array of challenges, thereby enhancing their problem-solving capabilities. This broader perspective can lead to innovative solutions, as individuals draw on knowledge from various fields to address complex issues. The act of enhancing one's performance through continuous improvement cannot be overstated. As individuals acquire new knowledge and skills, they refine their existing capabilities, resulting in increased efficiency and productivity. Such growth not only boosts individual confidence but also fosters motivation, as tangible progress becomes evident.

Innovation, too, is a significant byproduct of a culture rooted in continuous learning. By persistently seeking new knowledge and questioning established ideas, individuals can cultivate fresh perspectives and solutions that may not have been previously considered. This creative thinking is crucial in a world that values innovation as a driver of success, as highlighted in discussions around the relationship between luck and success, where preparedness meets opportunity. Consequently, those who engage in continuous learning are not only better prepared to seize opportunities but also to create them.

The importance of adaptability cannot be understated in this dynamic environment. Individuals who resist change often find themselves at a disadvantage, while those who embrace continuous learning can navigate uncertainties with ease. Developing a growth mindset is integral to this adaptability. This mindset fosters resilience and determination, attributes that are vital for personal and professional development.

Furthermore, personal development and fulfillment are significant outcomes of continuous learning. Engaging in the process of acquiring new knowledge and skills not only contributes to personal growth but also instills a sense of accomplishment. This fulfillment serves as a strong motivator, encouraging individuals to continue their learning journey and pursue their passions with renewed vigor. In a competitive job market, the ability to demonstrate a commitment to self-improvement becomes a valuable asset.

- Utilizing mentorship and feedback for growth

Mentorship and feedback stand as pivotal mechanisms for fostering personal growth and development, intricately linked to the broader themes of talent, luck, and the multifaceted factors that influence success.

At the foundation of mentorship lies the invaluable perspective and guidance it offers. Engaging with a mentor allows individuals to navigate their journeys with the benefit of someone else's experience. This is particularly pertinent given the acknowledgment of luck's role in success; mentorship can serve as a strategic advantage that enhances the likelihood of serendipitous opportunities. Mentors, through their own narratives, provide insights that empower mentees to make informed decisions, thereby steering them clear of potential pitfalls and enabling them to recognize and seize opportunities when they arise.

Moreover, mentorship significantly broadens networks and opens doors to new opportunities. A mentor's established professional connections can be a gateway for mentees to enter new realms of possibility. This expansion of one's professional network is not merely about social capital; it fundamentally alters the landscape of possibilities available to a mentee, enhancing their potential for growth.

Feedback, another crucial element of mentorship, fosters a culture of continuous learning. The constructive feedback provided by mentors allows mentees to gain critical insights into their strengths and weaknesses, creating a pathway for targeted improvement. This feedback loop is vital in honing one's skills and abilities, as it encourages individuals to refine their approach and elevate their performance.

Furthermore, mentorship plays a vital role in building confidence and self-efficacy. The encouragement and support that mentors provide can significantly bolster a mentee's belief in their own capabilities. This relationship nurtures a growth mindset, where challenges are reframed as opportunities for learning rather than obstacles.

Accountability also emerges as a crucial aspect of the mentorship dynamic. The structured environment that mentors create enables mentees to set realistic, achievable goals while fostering a sense of responsibility for their progress. This accountability mechanism is key in maintaining focus and motivation, allowing individuals to track their development over time.

Lastly, the emotional support offered by mentors cannot be overlooked. The journey of personal growth is often fraught with challenges that can evoke feelings of doubt and frustration. Mentorship provides a supportive framework, where mentors act as both guides and cheerleaders, helping mentees navigate difficult moments while celebrating their successes. This emotional reinforcement fosters resilience, enabling individuals to remain committed to their growth trajectories.

Chapter 8: The Intersection of Luck and Effort

Chapter 8.1: Timing and Preparation

The interplay of timing, preparation, luck, and effort forms a complex lattice that significantly influences individual success across various domains of life. Each of these factors plays a distinct yet interconnected role, often determining whether opportunities are seized or missed. Timing, in its essence, refers to the ability to recognize and act upon the right moment, which can be as pivotal as being in the right place at the right time. This notion of timing is intricately linked to the ability to discern emerging trends and the needs of the environment.

The synthesis of these two elements—timing and preparation—creates a fertile ground for success, where individuals can not only recognize opportunities but also have the requisite tools to exploit them effectively.

Effort is the final component that interlocks with timing, preparation, and luck to culminate in success. It embodies the dedication and tenacity required to pursue goals, confront challenges, and persist in the face of adversity. The realization of success is often underpinned by a consistent application of effort, which ensures that individuals remain engaged in the processes of timing and preparation. Effort acts as the driving force that propels individuals to translate their preparation into action, transforming potential opportunities into tangible outcomes.

To illustrate this intricate interplay, consider a hypothetical young entrepreneur who has dedicated years to preparing for the launch of a new product. Their preparation includes comprehensive market research, the development of a unique value proposition, and the establishment of a robust network of potential customers and partners. One fateful day, they attend a networking event where they fortuitously meet an influential investor eager to discover innovative ventures.

This chance meeting exemplifies luck, yet it is the entrepreneur's meticulous preparation and acute sense of timing that enable them to deliver a compelling pitch, ultimately securing the investment that propels their venture forward. Without the synergy of timing and preparation, this opportunity might have slipped through their fingers, underscoring the notion that luck alone cannot create success.

Moreover, risk management emerges as a critical factor in navigating the terrain of success. We introduced the metaphor of "green dots" representing opportunities and "red dots" symbolizing potential setbacks. By consciously minimizing exposure to red dots—whether through informed decision-making, fostering supportive networks, or making healthier lifestyle choices—individuals can enhance their ability to identify and engage with green dots, effectively increasing their likelihood of success.

Integrating these habits into daily routines not only fosters personal growth but also positions individuals to capitalize on the serendipity that may arise.

Chapter 8.2: Personal Anecdotes and Interviews

Let's provide a tapestry of personal anecdotes and interviews that underscore the intricate interplay between luck and effort in the journeys of successful individuals. The stories shared within this chapter serve not only as engaging narratives but also as profound reflections on how chance encounters and serendipitous moments can significantly shape one's career trajectory.

One interviewee recounts a pivotal moment during their senior year of college when, uncertain about their future, they stumbled upon an opportunity with Drexel Burnham Lambert, an investment bank. Their journey began not merely through diligent preparation but also through what they describe as a moment of luck—a chance interview that opened doors they had not anticipated. This personal anecdote illustrates how success can often hinge on being in the right place at the right time, a theme echoed throughout the chapter.

Another interviewee reflects on their experiences with chance events, contemplating whether they possess an innate sensitivity to these occurrences or if their observations are simply heightened compared to others. This introspective exploration leads to a broader realization that society tends to underestimate the influence of luck in shaping life outcomes. Such reflections challenge the conventional belief that success is solely the product of hard work and talent. Instead, they prompt readers to consider how often unseen forces may contribute to their achievements and failures alike.

The concept of luck is further illuminated by an interviewee who proudly identifies as the "luckiest person in the room." They attribute much of their success to being in the right circumstances, such as their educational opportunities and personal relationships. However, they also acknowledge a nuanced understanding of success that recognizes the hard work of others who may not have encountered the same fortuity.

As readers engage with these narratives, several critical lessons emerge. Moreover, the narratives emphasize that success cannot be solely attributed to personal attributes or characteristics. The tendency to equate success with meritocracy is challenged, suggesting that a more equitable distribution of resources and opportunities is necessary in society.

Chapter 9: Managing Anxiety Related to Unpredictability

In the contemporary landscape, where unpredictability has become a hallmark of daily life, the imperative to manage anxiety stemming from such uncertainty cannot be overstated. The emotional turmoil often triggered by the unknown can become a formidable barrier to personal and professional growth, yet there exist a plethora of strategies designed to alleviate these feelings and foster resilience. By examining such techniques, alongside the power of mindfulness and the inspiring narratives of those who have thrived amidst uncertainty, we can cultivate a robust framework for coping with anxiety.

Reframing thoughts stands out as a particularly effective strategy for managing anxiety related to unpredictability. This cognitive technique involves shifting one's perspective to view uncertainty not merely as a source of stress but as a fertile ground for growth and learning. By embracing this adaptive mindset, individuals can mitigate feelings of anxiety and approach the unknown with curiosity rather than trepidation. This aligns with the notion that effective communication and understanding of one's audience—be it in writing or in navigating interpersonal relationships—are vital in overcoming the barriers presented by doubt and fear.

Self-care emerges as another essential component in the quest to manage anxiety. Engaging in activities that nurture both physical and mental health—such as exercise, hobbies, and quality time with loved ones—serves to bolster resilience. The act of prioritizing self-care not only alleviates stress but also fosters a sense of agency, empowering individuals to reclaim control in an unpredictable world. Furthermore, integrating mindfulness practices into daily routines can profoundly impact emotional well-being. By anchoring oneself in the present moment, practitioners of mindfulness can observe their anxious thoughts with detachment, allowing for a more constructive response to their emotional landscape.

The interplay between mindfulness and resilience-building is particularly noteworthy. Mindfulness cultivates a heightened awareness of thoughts and feelings, enabling individuals to engage with their internal experiences without judgment. This practice fosters resilience by instilling the capacity to adapt to adversity and navigate uncertainty with a steady mindset. Additionally, adopting a growth mindset—one that sees challenges as opportunities rather than obstacles—can significantly enhance resilience. This perspective encourages individuals to view setbacks as integral to the journey of growth, thereby enabling them to rise from difficulties with renewed strength.

In contemplating the power of personal narratives, we find that stories of those who have triumphed over uncertainty serve as profound sources of inspiration. Take the example of Thomas Edison, whose relentless pursuit of innovation in developing the light bulb exemplifies resilience in the face of failure. Edison's perspective—that each failure was merely a step closer to success—highlights the importance of reframing setbacks as learning opportunities.

Ultimately, the ability to manage anxiety related to unpredictability and build resilience is an invaluable skill in navigating the complexities of modern life. By employing techniques such as reframing thoughts, embracing self-care, practicing mindfulness, and drawing strength from the stories of resilient individuals, we can cultivate a robust inner framework to face the unknown. These strategies remind us that our true strength often emerges from the depths of uncertainty, revealing our capacity to adapt, learn, and thrive. In this journey, it is essential to recognize that while external circumstances may be unpredictable, our mindset and resilience can illuminate the path forward, allowing us to navigate life's uncertainties with confidence and grace.

Chapter 10: Finding Fulfillment Amidst Uncertainty

Life presents itself as an intricate tapestry of unpredictability, where the only constant is change. To navigate this complexity effectively and emerge with resilience requires a multifaceted approach grounded in several key insights. Recognizing that many setbacks in life stem from factors beyond our control is a vital first step. Often, we fall prey to the misconception that every misfortune is a direct reflection of our abilities or decisions. In reality, life can hurl unforeseen challenges our way; thus, one effective strategy is to minimize risks in our daily choices.

Equally important is the cultivation of meaningful interactions with others. Social connections extend beyond mere companionship; they can serve as valuable resources for knowledge and support. By engaging with our communities, we not only foster relationships that can open doors to new opportunities but also glean insights from others' experiences, enabling us to avoid potential pitfalls. In this sense, knowledge acts as a protective shield against the unpredictability of life, turning our social networks into a safety net.

However, it is crucial to recognize that the journey through life's unpredictability is not uniform for everyone. The insights derived from this journey indicate that socio-economic factors significantly influence one's experiences. Acknowledging our own privilege is essential. Also understanding that not everyone enjoys the same opportunities.

Another paramount aspect of navigating life's challenges is the power of perspective. Life's unpredictability can indeed be overwhelming, yet by consciously choosing to shift our perspective, we can reframe setbacks as opportunities for growth. This perspective not only strengthens our coping mechanisms but also transforms obstacles into stepping stones.

Finding joy and purpose in a world characterized by uncertainty and unpredictable outcomes is undoubtedly a challenge that many grapple with.

We do possess the ability to influence our perceptions and responses. By adopting a positive mindset and consciously seeking out the silver linings in difficult situations, we can uncover opportunities for joy even amidst uncertainty.

Nassim Taleb, a prominent risk analyst, argues that the unpredictability of life plays a crucial role in success. In his seminal work "The Black Swan," he elucidates the impact of rare, unforeseen events that shape our lives and endeavors. Taleb advocates for a mindset that not only acknowledges but welcomes uncertainty, suggesting that the ability to adapt to unexpected outcomes is essential for thriving in a volatile environment.

Michael Mauboussin further explores the intricate relationship between luck and skill, particularly in fields where outcomes are heavily influenced by unpredictable factors, such as financial trading. His research underscores the necessity of distinguishing between what is within our control and what is not. By acknowledging the substantial role of chance in success, individuals can make more informed decisions, blending skill with an acceptance of uncertainty.

Similarly, John's experience as a professional athlete highlights the critical role of a positive mindset in overcoming adversity. After a career-threatening injury, John could have easily given in to uncertainty and doubt. Instead, he embraced the challenge, dedicating himself to rehabilitation and fostering a belief in his eventual comeback. His story serves as a powerful reminder that setbacks can become opportunities for growth when approached with determination and a willingness to adapt.

In synthesizing these narratives, we recognize that embracing uncertainty is not synonymous with reckless decision-making. Rather, it involves cultivating a mindset that welcomes change, learns from setbacks, and seeks out opportunities amid chaos.

Chapter 11: Replicating Success and Overcoming Obstacles

Through my extensive research, I have identified that certain commonalities emerge among those who achieve repeat successes across various fields. Personal characteristics, such as talent and skill, indeed play a significant role; however, they do not encompass the entirety of what drives success. The interplay between these attributes and other elements is crucial for a comprehensive understanding of achievement in any arena, including sports, arts, and sciences.

Moreover, the paradox of skill elucidates the intricate relationship between skill and luck. As one's skill level enhances, the significance of luck tends to increase, particularly in disciplines where both factors are pivotal. This concept, as articulated by biologist Stephen Jay Gould, finds a vivid illustration in the career of Ted Williams, the legendary baseball player renowned for being the last to hit over 400 in Major League Baseball. Williams's experience underscores the idea that heightened skill does not eliminate the role of luck but rather amplifies it, challenging the common misconception that skill alone guarantees success.

My findings also reveal distinct recurring patterns in successful ventures that provide valuable insights for aspiring entrepreneurs. One prominent pattern is the crucial role of passion and perseverance. Individuals who are deeply passionate about their endeavors and exhibit resilience in the face of adversity are more likely to navigate challenges effectively and achieve their objectives. This unwavering dedication serves as a cornerstone of their success.

Additionally, the presence of imagination and intellectual curiosity is another vital pattern. Successful individuals are characterized by their eagerness to explore new ideas and their willingness to remain open to innovative thinking. This curiosity allows them to recognize unique opportunities and devise groundbreaking solutions, thereby positioning themselves advantageously within their respective fields.

Timing is equally pivotal, as it dictates the optimal moments to act upon opportunities that arise. A venture's ability to recognize and respond to market trends and customer needs can significantly differentiate it from its competitors. The nuances of timing require a balance of proactivity and patience, where ventures must be vigilant observers of their environments to capitalize on fleeting opportunities while avoiding unnecessary haste that could lead to missteps.

Adaptability emerges as a critical factor in navigating the complexities of an ever-evolving landscape. In a world characterized by rapid change, the capacity to pivot in response to new challenges and shifts in market dynamics can determine a venture's survival. Those that embrace innovation and are willing to experiment with new approaches are better positioned to thrive amidst uncertainty. This adaptability is not simply a reactive measure; it entails an ongoing commitment to learning and evolution, which is essential for maintaining relevance in a competitive marketplace.

Importantly, these factors are not isolated; they are interdependent and mutually reinforcing. A sound strategy inherently considers timing and the necessity for adaptability, thereby allowing ventures to navigate the complexities of their respective fields more adeptly.

A well-articulated strategy serves as the guiding principle for these individuals, akin to a North Star that directs their efforts amidst the tumultuous landscape of business challenges. They recognize that a clear roadmap is essential for making informed decisions, setting achievable goals, and effectively allocating resources, thereby allowing them to maintain focus on their long-term vision even when confronted with uncertainties.

Interestingly, while these individuals prioritize strategy, timing, and adaptability, they also recognize the serendipitous role of luck in their journeys. Rather than relying solely on chance, they leverage fortunate circumstances as catalysts for further success. Their preparedness positions them to seize opportunities that arise unexpectedly, reinforcing the adage that luck favors the prepared.

Ultimately, the lessons distilled from the experiences of serial entrepreneurs and innovators underscore the significance of a well-defined strategy, the critical nature of timing, and the necessity of adaptability in achieving enduring success. By assimilating these insights into our own pursuits, we not only enhance our chances of accomplishing our goals but also position ourselves to make meaningful contributions to our respective fields.

Don't miss out!

Visit the website below and you can sign up to receive emails whenever Joseph Hover publishes a new book. There's no charge and no obligation.

https://books2read.com/r/B-A-OZRIB-RMOBF

BOOKS 2 READ

Connecting independent readers to independent writers.

Did you love *How Lucky Are You? Deconstructing the Myth of Meritocracy, Hard Work and Winning in Life*? Then you should read *The Case Against Procreation: Antinatalism in Modern Discourse*[1] by Joseph Hover!

[2]

In "The Case Against Procreation", Joseph Hover presents a provocative and deeply researched critique of the most fundamental aspect of human society: having children. Through a series of compelling arguments and insightful analyses, this book makes the case for antinatalism, the philosophical position that it is morally wrong to procreate.

Through its rigorous and accessible exploration of the ethics and consequences of procreation, this book will challenge readers to rethink their assumptions about the value and purpose of having children. Is parenthood truly a selfless act, or is it a selfish desire driven by personal fulfillment and social pressure? Can we truly justify bringing new life into a world plagued by suffering, inequality, and environmental degradation?

---

1. https://books2read.com/u/4jMvrk

2. https://books2read.com/u/4jMvrk